Getting Started in

PROPERTY FLIPPING

The *Getting Started In* Series

Getting Started in
PROPERTY FLIPPING

Michael C. Thomsett

John Wiley & Sons, Inc.

Published by John Wiley & Sons, Inc., Hoboken, New Jersey.

Published simultaneously in Canada.

For general information on our other products and services or for technical support, please contact our Customer Care Department within the United States at (800) 762-2974, outside the United States at (317) 572-3993 or fax (317) 572-4002.

Wiley also publishes its books in a variety of electronic formats. Some content that appears in print may not be available in electronic books. For more information about Wiley products, visit our website at www.wiley.com.

Library of Congress Cataloging-in-Publication Data
Thomsett, Michael C.
  Getting started in property flipping / Michael C. Thomsett.
    p. cm.
  Includes index.
  ISBN-13: 978-0-470-03937-3 (pbk.)
  ISBN-10: 0-470-03937-X (pbk.)
  1. Real estate investment. 2. House buying 3. House selling. I. Title.
  HD1382.5.T563 2007
  332.63'24—dc22

                              2006013973

Printed in the United States of America.

10 9 8 7 6 5 4 3 2 1

Contents

Chapter 8

Chapter 9

Chapter 10

The Not-So-Typical Approach to Real Estate

O f the many ways to buy real estate, property flipping is the most creative. It solves several of the problems faced by traditional investors—and it presents entirely new ones.

Most investors typically think of real estate investing in standard equity modes: You offer a down payment on a single property, get approval for financing, and hold on to the property while waiting for it to appreciate in value. If the value grows quickly, you profit from the investment. If growth is slow, however, it is the lender who makes more profit from interest than you do from ownership.

This is the single greatest problem in outright ownership of property. Lenders often realize more profit than investors—and without the problems and costs of dealing with tenants; paying insurance, taxes, utilities, and maintenance; and contending with ever-changing demand in the market.

Investors in the past have avoided the problems of equity ownership by buying in investment pools such as the pooled funds of Ginnie and Fannie Maes, the Government National Mortgage Association (GNMA) and the Federal National Mortgage Association (FNMA), respectively. These government agencies collected the pool of secured residential property mortgages, bundled them together, and sold units in increments of $5,000 or more. Because all of the mortgages are secured in this pool, risks are low. But unlike an equity position, investors own a piece of a larger debt pool. Other pooled investments have included limited partnerships in which losses cannot be claimed on tax returns but must be carried over and applied against future passive activity gains. For that reason, real estate limited partnerships are not as attractive as they were in the past. Finally, investors can purchase shares of real estate investment trusts (REITs). These operate like other pools in the sense that investors' money is placed together to buy, mortgage, or build large-scale properties such as shopping centers or industrial parks. REIT shares are traded over public stock exchanges just like stocks, solving the liquidity problems usually found in other kinds of real estate.

An alternative does exist, one that is more interesting and potentially more profitable: property flipping. In this approach, you buy property that is most likely to appreciate in value over the short term. This property is held and sold as quickly as possible. In some variations of the strategy, several cosmetic repairs are performed and then the property is sold. Which variation is right for you depends on your comfort zone or, more accurately, your "risk tolerance."

This book is aimed at the investor looking for ways to expand his or her product horizons in real estate, especially for the first time. It is not intended as a comprehensive text for advanced and experienced property flipping professionals—but it does open the door for you. You may be comfortable with stocks, mutual funds, residential real estate through home ownership or limited landlord activity, and with other methods for allocating your assets.

You may also want to get in on the strong real estate market—or simply want to speculate with some of your capital.

Of course, the real estate "bubble" that has been around for many years will eventually burst. But you need to know that it is not likely to burst everywhere at the same time. Unlike stocks, whose values tend to be universal, real estate values are completely local in nature. So trends in Phoenix are not affected by changes in Florida or New York. Each region is defined separately and by its own demographic and economic characteristics. The supply and demand in real estate varies considerably between regions. No single changes in the economy affect every market in the same way or at the same time.

Also, a large part of the bubble has been upheld by low interest rates. If those rates change in either direction, there would be a natural change in many regions as well. But real estate investors also recognize that beyond interest rates, more factors affect value. It does little good to invest in low-interest loans in an area where no jobs exist and where property values are falling. It does a lot of good to still invest, even when rates are high, where you know that conditions are going to be ripe for values to rise. Wise property flipping depends on a thorough knowledge about your area's market—and that is just the starting point.

This book shows you how to start by explaining the many sides of property flipping. It takes you through the process of defining whether flipping is appropriate for you. It also shows how various strategies can be used, how you approach valuation of property, and the resources and experts you need to work with to ensure that the strategies work. Property flipping, like all forms of real estate investment, requires working with the right people, getting the best information, and gaining knowledge of your own to better locate property flipping opportunities.

The property flipping market is nothing new. It has been around for years, as speculators have recognized the potential for profit in expanding markets. Today, with so many different kinds of real estate markets, it is more important than ever to know when and where property flipping works. With the right background, you too can have a profitable experience.

—Michael C. Thomsett

Getting Started in

PROPERTY FLIPPING

From Their Money to Yours

Leverage and Cash Flow

The concept of *property flipping* is not new and has been around for a very long time. As a form of *speculation*, flipping involves moving into an ownership position and then selling at a profit, sometimes in a very short period of time. In fact, the time element is most crucial in all real estate investments. The longer the holding period, the more critical the question of *cash flow* becomes. A flipper, by definition, is a very short-term investor.

The property flipper believes that an undervalued property's profit is maximized through the short-term period. Someone else may view an improved property as a viable long-term hold, either as a primary residence or as a rental; but the flipper is much more interested in the fast in-and-out of property flipping. Indeed, it is likely that the selection criteria for a flip property are entirely different than the criteria for a long-term growth prospect (owner-occupied or rental).

Flipping can certainly be applied to raw land as well as commercial and industrial property. However, in this book, the emphasis of discussion is limited to single-family residential property. This

property flipping

a form of speculation in real estate that involves a very short period of ownership. The flipper finds undervalued properties, improves value through cosmetic improvements in many instances, and then sells the property at a profit.

speculation

an investment strategy employed by short-term investors. These investors seek rapid turnover of investment funds as opposed to long-term investors, whose objectives are to buy and hold for many years.

cash flow

the movement of money in and out of an investment. In real estate, cash flow is of greater concern than ultimate profits. For example, speculators seek extremely short-term investments so that cash flow concerns are limited; therefore, they desire to sell properties as soon as possible after acquiring them.

is the type of property most investors emphasize; it is the most familiar; and market valuation, rental markets, and financing are more basic and straight-forward for residential real estate than for most other types.

Property flipping may include speculation in raw land and has always been a popular notion for real estate investors. In fact, even in the colonial period, property flipping on the American frontier was widespread. In those days, land ownership of-ten was defined by occupying the land and work-ing it, and not by actual title. Many squatters assumed ownership by farming land, but as time went on, speculators moved in, as explained by one historian:

Unlike the squatters, the speculators intended not to make homes on the frontier but merely to make money. Their strategy was to acquire title to large tracts of land, either directly from the Indians or, after that practice was out-lawed (because of the abuses it invited), from the colonial governments or from the British Crown. They then sent out surveyors, who mapped their holdings, and wrote up legal de-scriptions. Finally they sold the lands, ideally at a handsome profit, to settlers. [1]

This description of frontier-level speculation literally involved surveying and describing the land involved. Today, virtually all land has been surveyed

---

Key Point

Most property flipping strategies involve residential real estate, which has the greatest number of properties and the higher level of market activity. Other types of real estate should be left to the experts.

---

[1] H. W. Brands, *Andrew Jackson, His Life and Times* (New York: Doubleday, 2005), p. 14.

and plotted, and legal descriptions exist; so at least today's property flippers do not have to carve descriptions out of the wilderness. But the description of speculation in the late 18th century applies as well in the early 21st century. The strategy is the same: Find undervalued land, acquire it, and sell it at a profit as quickly as possible.

The Lifeblood of Property Flipping

Other people's money—descriptive of how *leverage* and cash flow work—is a reference to how most real estate investors operate. This is out of necessity. When you buy your first home, you borrow most of the money through a mortgage; this is a form of leverage, the use of other people's money. The cost of borrowing, interest, is a long-term burden to every homeowner who needs a 30-year mortgage.

> **leverage**
> an investment strategy in which a portion of equity is augmented through borrowings to purchase more expensive items than the investor could afford in cash. In real estate, mortgage loans are the best-known form of leverage.

By the same argument, real estate investors almost always have to employ leverage to take up equity positions in real estate. Few people have enough cash available to avoid leverage. An important reality every investor needs to face is that leverage is accompanied by risk. The more leverage employed, the greater this *cash flow risk* will be, and this is unavoidable.

> **cash flow risk**
> a form of risk involving the use of leverage. The greater the leverage used in investments, the greater the cash flow risk.

The fact that leverage (and its advantages) is tied unavoidably to risk (and its disadvantages) is the essential problem for all real estate investors. The homeowner can only qualify for a loan if the lender believes the borrower's income is high enough to afford payments. Real estate investors

---

Key Point

Leverage is unavoidable in real estate. Most investors, like most homeowners, have to borrow the larger portion of the purchase price. *Affordability*, therefore, often refers more to managing monthly payments and expenses than to the stated purchase price of property.

Key Point

Those who consider property flipping too risky may prefer long-term holdings and working with tenants. That can be risky as well when potential cash flow problems are considered.

---

and their lenders assess borrowing in the same manner. The long-term investor, who probably will rent out the property, is concerned about whether market rents will be adequate to pay the mortgage as well as maintenance, property taxes, insurance, and other recurring costs associated with ownership. Because leverage determines the feasibility of such an investment, the landlord lives with the risk of high-ticket repairs, vacancies, nonpayment of rent, property tax increases, growing payments in adjustable rate mortgages, and any other factor affecting cash flow.

Every investor faces a multifaceted level of cash flow risk premised on the need to borrow money or to leverage the investment. At first glance, leverage is very attractive. A 20 percent down payment makes the investment look quite promising. By borrowing 80 percent, the capital invested goes much farther. Thus, even an investor with $200,000 to invest does not need to buy only one $200,000 house. It is "easy" on paper to buy five houses with 20 percent down and have $1 million in play. However, the problems of loan qualification and cash flow tend to curtail the extent of potential leverage; and reality itself (in the form of vacancies, unexpected costs, and other cash flow problems) increases risk, and can make the "sure thing" not so sure after all.

The concept of leveraging money is illustrated in Figure 1.1. Here, $200,000 is used to purchase five properties, each with 20 percent down. If all five properties were to double in value, leverage would produce greater profits than could be realized in buying only a single property—assuming, that is, that the profit can be realized before interest costs consume that profit.

Key Point

Leverage is an exciting idea when you realize how a small amount of money can work for you—at least on paper. A more in-depth study is essential.

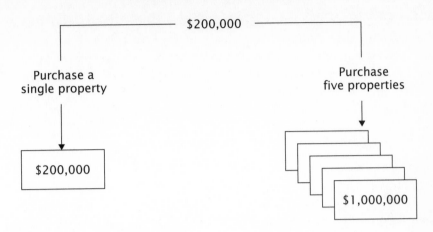

FIGURE 1.1 Leveraging Money

For example, look at what occurs if property values increase by 20 percent over one year (assuming average interest of 8 percent on all properties):

	Buying a single property for cash	*Buying five properties financed at 8%*
Purchase price	$200,000	$1,000,000
Profit, 20%	40,000	200,000
Appreciated value	$240,000	$1,200,000
Less: interest	0	–64,000
Net	$240,000	$1,136,000

Interest was calculated at 8 percent of $800,000 (overall property value of $1,000,000 minus $200,000 down payments). This illustration shows the power of leverage, but also assumes that all properties would be sold at the end of the one-year period. There is always the risk that property values will not grow at the rate or, for that matter, at all.

The *risk* involved with leverage involves management of cash flow. You need to assume that, in the ownership of five leveraged properties, there will be enough cash coming in from rents or appreciated market value to pay the mortgage payments. If that plan is not realized, the cash flow risk can make the venture expensive.

When the cash flow risks are considered in the overall scheme of things, many investors are discouraged from pursuing the most common real estate investment paths. Owning single-family homes and renting them out involves many types of risk, not the least of which is cash flow risk. So some people have preferred to invest in real estate partnerships or real estate investment trusts (REITs), where risks are spread and properties are managed by professional developers, builders, and investors. REIT shares are traded on public exchanges, so this course is far more liquid than direct ownership of property. Some investors have also chosen to take a debt position rather than an equity position, and invested in mortgage pools. These are similar in structure to mortgage funds, but portfolios consist of residential mortgages rather than stocks or bonds.

Finally, the property flipping alternative deserves a serious look as well. Because flipping is designed to work as a short-term strategy in real estate, the longer-term cash flow risk can be avoided and remains out of the equation. Exceptions may occur. You might enter a transaction intending to flip and later decide to hold the property for the longer term and rent it out. As a rule, however, the transaction is going to be designed to create a profit as quickly as possible, thus avoiding having to include cash flow risk in the equation. So for property flippers, the feasibility of a particular transaction is different than it is for buy-and-hold strategies. This is an essential point to keep in mind: Because the risk factors and assumptions are different between flipping and holding, you need to analyze a specific property using an appropriate set of criteria that matches the strategy properly.

market risk

the best-known type of investment risk—that prices will fall after money has been invested. Market (or price) risk applies in all markets. In real estate, the combination of market risk with timing often defines whether investments succeed or fail.

Opportunity and Risk in Leverage

Leverage itself can be viewed as a two-sided coin: opportunity on one side and risk on the other. This relationship cannot be avoided or mitigated. The greater the opportunity for profits, the greater the corresponding risk. The risk will be present in one form or another. Of the various types of risk, *market risk* is the best known; but cash flow risk growing out of leverage is equally serious. If the property does not increase in value in the short term, you have to wait out that market. If interest rates rise and you have financed property with an adjustable rate mortgage, your costs continue to climb. If the

---

Key Point

Most investors concentrate on market price and associated risks. In real estate, though, cash flow risk is at least as critical and should be studied carefully as part of your analysis.

---

demand for rentals becomes soft, a higher rate of vacancies will erode your cash flow.

The relationship between opportunity and risk is summarized in Figure 1.2. Note that if these two elements are charted in degrees, opportunity and risk tend to move in the same direction and usually at the same rate of change.

A mistake made by investors in all markets is to overlook this relationship between opportunity and risk. The tendency is to focus on the profit potential of an investment but to forget about the corresponding risk. This does not mean it is impossible to make a profit in real estate; but real estate investors accept specific types of risks as a trade-off for the opportunity.

The same is true in the stock market. Highly volatile stocks are likely to increase in value over the short term far more so than lower-volatility stocks. But that price can also move downward with equal speed and degree. So a very conservative investor will prefer stocks with little volatility and accept a lower overall return on their investment—a trade-off for safety and certainty with lower profits so as to avoid risk and uncertainty and the possibility of higher profit potential.

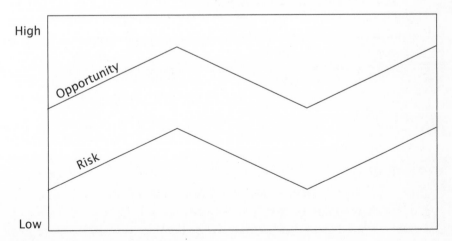

FIGURE 1.2 Opportunity and Risk

suitability
the appropriate matching of a particular investment strategy to an individual, based on experience, knowledge, income, assets, investment goals, age, and family status.

Managing risk in any investment portfolio is a matter of matching that risk to individual tolerance. For this reason, it makes sense to begin the process of studying property flipping by asking yourself: *Is this an appropriate avenue for me to pursue?*

Not everyone is suited for property flipping. Just as some stock market investors prefer strongly capitalized blue chip stocks, others are attracted to new issues, options or futures, and other more exotic (and higher-risk) market alternatives. *Suitability* is determined by several factors, including:

1. *Experience and knowledge.* If you are experienced in real estate investing and know the range of market risks, that is an important first step. You also need to be very familiar with real estate trends in your area, because those trends determine the strength or weakness of the market, today and tomorrow. Every market is different. There are few similarities between Manhattan and the Florida panhandle, for example; or between San Francisco and Colorado Springs. So the coupling of experience and knowledge define suitability for higher-risk investing.

2. *Income and assets.* You cannot afford to place capital at risk if you cannot afford a loss. So the overall value of your investment assets, plus annual income, are going to limit and define what you will be able to include in your portfolio. If you are barely making your family budget on today's income, you cannot afford to speculate in real estate. If your credit is poor, you will be at a disadvantage as well, because your ability to obtain favorable financing terms will be crucial. In addition to income and personal cash flow, your assets will also determine the suitability of property flipping.

Key Point

Every real estate market is regional. National trends may be interesting, but they do not apply to *your* city or town.

3. *Investment goals.* People invest for different reasons. Some want to accumulate wealth so that they can retire early. Others want to pay off their house, fund a child's college education, or start a business. Other people simply want to create financial security for themselves. Your goals and personal priorities should determine what kinds of investments are most appropriate for you. The range is wide. Insurance or annuities, conservative stocks and bonds, mutual funds, speculative stocks, derivatives, and many forms of real estate are all among the possible choices. Ultimately, your investment goals need to be foremost in how and why you pick one investment over another.

4. *Your personal opinion and point of view.* You may have a particular bias toward one type of investment, or against it. The reasons vary, but the fact remains that everyone makes their own judgment calls. It does not make sense to try and convince someone to change their bias. For example, if you are suspicious about the stock market, it is not likely that anyone will be able to convince you that your money should be invested in stocks. And if you believe that real estate is the only truly safe investment, it will be equally difficult to dissuade you. So the investments you choose will reflect your own beliefs.

5. *Age and family status.* Finally, you are likely to decide upon investing in one or more products based on your age and family status. Younger investors are more likely to take chances with their money, so they may be attracted to more speculative investments. As people grow older, they tend to become more conservative in their choices. Single people can afford to take greater risks as well. When people get married their priorities change; married people may want to buy a home and start a family, which means that investments have to be made more cautiously as well.

Ultimately, your decision to invest money anywhere should be based on research and full understanding of the risks involved, and not just the profit potential. The suitability of an investment or range of investments or strategies should be determined by analysis and comparison. Knowing the risk attributes of investments—especially real estate—requires becoming aware of the economic, demographic, and market factors of real estate in your city or town. Real estate is always

---

Key Point

You read a lot of general advice: You *should* invest today to beat the market, you *should* buy real estate now, or you *should* leverage your money. But in practice, everyone is different, and a course of action is best determined by your circumstances, and not by general advice.

---

local in nature, so no national averages are of any use in this research. Just as the Dow Jones Industrial Averages (DJIA) cannot identify the value of any one stock, national real estate averages provide useful information about broad trends, but they are meaningless in terms of the market where you live.

Leverage and Risk Analysis

Many leverage illustrations discuss how a limited amount of money can be applied to control multiple properties. This is the essence of leverage, of course. However, the emphasis on maximizing the use of money ignores the equally important element of risk. The greater the leverage, the greater the cash flow risk. When you leverage money, you cannot escape this risk, and a thorough analysis should include equating the advantages with that *liquidity risk*.

liquidity risk
a form of risk involving cash flow and the availability of money. The risk is based on the need for regular income from investment real estate to make mortgage payments, ongoing expenses, and unexpected repairs. The greater the leverage employed in a real estate portfolio, the higher the liquidity risk.

When you analyze an idea for investing in real estate (whether a single property or a number of properties), your analysis may include a number of review "points"—supply and demand, local vacancy rates, growth rates, and so on. These market analyses may be thought of as the fundamentals of real estate analysis. Just as stock investors study financial statements and track ratios to make judgments about corporations and their stocks, real estate investors can also study valuation and market potential.

Some stock investors also look at the technical side, the price movement and volatility of a stock. Real estate investors may do the same by studying attributes of price and market value; but in real estate, you also need to include cash flow in this technical analysis. In real estate, the equivalent of stock-based technical analysis has to include all price-related elements because, ultimately, these will also define the level of cash flow risk.

The asked price of a property (or average prices in your city) is not necessarily revealing about the strength or weakness of the market from a technical point of view; you need to find out more. Six elements of this analysis include:

1. *Cash flow "worst case" analysis.* A study of cash flow is intended to estimate the cash you receive from renting out property versus the cash you have to pay for mortgage obligations, property taxes, insurance, utilities, maintenance, and any major repairs. In its "worst case" form, the unknown risks can threaten the feasibility of your investment. You need to ensure that you can afford these unexpected surprises, including vacancies, nonpayment or late payment of rent, and major repairs.

    These potential problems certainly affect cash flow. Many investors perform an overly optimistic cash flow analysis. They assume rents will be received every month, and no unknown surprises will occur. So as a critical segment of your real estate technical analysis, you also need to be aware of the exposure to cash flow risk as part of the equation. It is not enough to be aware of potential growth in market value and profits, if you also risk not being able to afford to keep properties as long as you need to.

2. *The spread.* The difference between the listed "for sale" price and the ultimate "sold" price is called the *spread.* Checking the spread and the trend in spread over the past year gives you a very good indication of the strength or weakness in the market. The information is available through a Multiple Listing Service (MLS) most real estate brokerages use, and which many local bankers also subscribe to. The computation of spread is performed for properties of each kind. So the average spread for all residential

---

Key Point

The use of technical analysis is well known in the stock market; it also has a specific application for real estate investors and can greatly improve your ability to judge today's market.

Key Point

The *spread*—equivalent to "bid and asked" prices—defines the market for real estate in terms of supply and demand. For that reason, spread is one of the more important market indicators to study.

---

properties is summarized by month for at least a full year. The computation involves dividing the difference between asked and sales price, by the asked price, and is expressed as a percentage:

$$\frac{\text{Asked price} - \text{Sales price}}{\text{Asked price}} = \text{Spread}$$

spread

the percentage of difference between asked and sold price of real estate. To compute, divide the difference in the two values by the asked price and express the result as a percentage.

The greater the spread, the softer the market. For example, if the trend has been for an increase in the spread (meaning final sales prices have been increasingly lower than asked prices) means the market is losing strength. As a spread decreases, it indicates growing strength in the market (also meaning that the demand is growing stronger). In exceptionally strong markets, the spread will be very small. This reflects many properties selling for prices above asked price, so that the average is reduced greatly.

3. *The "time on the market" trend.* Another technical indicator of market strength or weakness is the number of months or weeks that properties remain on the market. This *time on the market* trend is very revealing. In very strong markets, properties move quickly, selling in one month or less from the date of the original listing. Typically, in balanced markets, properties tend to sell between 30 and 90 days. In very weak markets (where more sellers exist than buyers) properties may remain on the market longer than 90 days, and many may be withdrawn from the market without a sale. Time on the market is tracked through MLS services, and information can be found through a local real estate brokerage firm.

time on the market

the number of months (or weeks) that properties remain for sale on average. This indicates the relative strength or weakness—and the recent changes in time on the market indicate a trend in supply and demand.

4. *Inventory of properties for sale, expressed in time.* The current *inventory of properties* available for sale reveals how much turnover is occurring in today's local real estate market. The inventory represents the number of months of properties available. So if history shows that 25 properties sell per month, when 100 homes are currently listed, that is a four-month inventory of properties; if 300 properties are currently listed, that is a full 12-month-supply. The lower the inventory, the stronger the market.

> **inventory of properties**
> the number of properties currently listed and for sale divided by the average number of sales per month in a specific region or city; the lower the inventory, the stronger the market.

5. *Real estate price trends in the local market.* The most basic type of analysis of real estate is based on price. While that is only a part of the picture, it is an essential part. If you cannot afford the investment, the entire exercise is useless. In addition, you also must ensure that other price-related elements make sense. For property flipping, you must ensure that the trend in the market is likely to ensure a profit in the short term. For longer-term investing, it is equally important to ensure that the levels of market rents are adequate to cover mortgage payments and other recurring expenses. This is not always possible. In some markets, real estate prices are relatively high but rental rates may not be adequate to cover cash flow demands.

Price alone is only one piece of the price puzzle. Of more importance is the *price trend* in local real estate. This is the typical, or average, range of prices for properties like ones you are considering buying. If you are interested in three-bedroom, two-bath homes with 2,000 square feet, then you narrow your analysis to homes generally fitting that description. Based on specific neighborhood characteristics, you can identify the price trend for

---

Key Point

Even property flippers need to be aware of trends in rental supply and demand—because that also affects real estate values and can signal the near-term price direction.

price trend

the historical prices of properties in a particular area, involving a period of 12 months or more. The trend is useful in judging how real estate prices are moving currently, and to anticipate future price ranges.

the kind of property involved. Even within one city, prices can and do vary considerably by neighborhood, even when close together. The actual or perceived value is going to be affected by numerous factors, some of which are simply known to those familiar with the market. Thus, it may take time to acquire the knowledge about local real estate that cannot be learned from MLS listings, analysis, or a study of the numbers. In some cases, you learn more by talking to other people in your city, those you meet over coffee or at the post office. Understanding the subtleties of local price trends is not always limited to pure analysis.

6. *Rental demand trends.* An entirely separate real estate "market" exists in the form of *rental demand.* This has to be reviewed separately from price trends, because it does not necessarily match. A broad assumption (which might be wrong) is that a strong overall residential demand will be matched by an equally strong rental demand. The two markets coexist but react to entirely separate market forces. Homeowners and renters are *not* the same demographic. The relative strength of one form of demand over the other depends on the local job market, demographic mix (college-aged renters versus homeowners and retirees), and prices. It is possible that real estate prices have grown substantially, but rental demand is weak (due, perhaps, to overbuilding apartments in the area), or that rental demand is very strong but real estate prices are weak (due, for example, to a large college population and overbuilding single-family housing).

rental demand

the specific demand market for rentals affected by the supply of rental houses and apartments. This market coexists with the larger housing market with its pricing trends; but renters react to different factors than homeowners, so the two markets may not necessarily move in the same direction.

Leverage and Other Types of Risk

If you view leverage as a specific type of risk, you can analyze its attributes wisely. As with all forms of risk, leverage contains both

Key Point
Leverage risk is specific, but the use of leverage also defines other forms of risk. Real estate analysis is more reliably performed with this in mind.

potential and risk, and these aspects need to be offset against one another in order to appreciate how real estate is bought and sold; how to manage your personal investment risks; and how to set a time frame for property flipping itself. For example, the *ideal* time frame might be to turn property over as quickly as possible, but in some circumstances you might be willing to keep a short-term equity position to maximize profit potential (while accepting a limited leverage risk during the same period).

So leverage risk needs to be analyzed as a specific type of risk involved in any type of financed real estate purchase. At the same time, leverage also has to be considered with five other types of risk:

1. *Debt and equity risk.* Every investor chooses to adopt either an equity or a debt risk. Equity investors in real estate almost always use leverage because real estate is a big-ticket item. Exceptions are some forms of extremely short-term flipping; purchase of REIT shares; purchase of limited partnership units; or purchase of real estate *exchange-traded funds* (ETFs).

   The debt investor lends money to others, directly or through a *pooled investment* of some kind. Among these are bond funds and mortgage pools—called "Ginnie Maes" and "Fannie Maes"—offered by such quasi-government agencies as the Government National Mortgage Association (GNMA) or Federal National Mortgage Association (FNMA).

exchange-traded funds (ETFs) mutual funds with preidentified portfolios specializing in an industry or investing in stocks of a particular region or country. An ETF specializing in real estate companies offers one way of diversified equity investing without the use of leverage. ETF shares are traded over public exchanges, rather than bought or sold through the mutual fund itself.

pooled investment
an investment with the funds of many individuals combined to make purchases collectively, much like a mutual fund. Mortgage pools invest in bundles of secured real estate mortgages and are offered to the public by quasi-governmental agencies such as GNMA and FNMA.

interest risk
the risk that interest rates will rise, which has an immediate effect on real estate values. Higher interest rates also affect property flipping because higher rates slow down the market.

2. *Basic market risk.* The market risk every investor faces is complex in real estate, because a single market is not involved. When you buy shares of stock, the share value either rises or falls; in real estate, you have to consider the overall market risk relating to the value of property, *and* the risks associated with the rental market. Your market risk concerning rental supply and demand is entirely separate from the better understood market risk and, in some markets, may define success or failure. The risk itself comes down to one potential problem: that low rental demand may negatively impact cash flow even when market values are rising.

3. *Interest risk.* Investors in all markets are affected by changing interest rates and none more so than real estate investors. Because most investors depend so heavily on mortgage financing, *interest risk* is always present. This affects profit potential in more ways than one. The traditional purchase-and-hold strategy involves fixed or variable rates, so that any increase in interest curtails the market broadly. Higher rates create a more limited pool of potential buyers. Because payments grow higher with increased rates, more people cannot qualify for loans. Ultimately, the restricted market may also affect growth in market value. So the higher interest rates move, the *lower* the demand, and the lower the profit potential in investment real estate. This will have a direct impact on property flipping, which thrives best in a rapidly growing value environment.

Key Point

Interest risk is not limited to changing rates; higher rates create less demand because fewer potential buyers can qualify for financing.

4. *Diversification and asset allocation risk.* An ever-present problem for investors is management of investment capital to achieve *diversification* among several different products. Diversification comes in many forms; stock investors diversify by investing in mutual funds, and direct purchase of stocks usually involves several dissimilar stocks. Real estate investors diversify by buying different properties or mixing property types. An expanded aspect of diversification is *asset allocation*, which means placing capital in different markets (stocks, bonds, and real estate, for example) so that no one poor performing market affects the entire portfolio. The risk in both diversification and allocation is that it may not be done effectively. For example, if a stock investor buys four or five different stocks, that is one form of diversification; but if all of those stocks would react in the same way to bad economic news, then diversification is not achieved. The same risk applies to asset allocation. If you allocate your portfolio between directly owned stocks and mutual funds, a marketwide bear market will affect your whole portfolio. If you allocate between residential property and raw land, a regional softness in *all* real estate would apply to the entire portfolio and, again, the allocation would not be effective. So investors in all markets face the risk that their diversification and allocation strategies might not be effective. This demands constant reevaluation of the strategy itself based on current economic and market conditions.

diversification
a strategy for spreading risk, in which investment capital is placed in dissimilar products. The purpose of diversification is to ensure that bad news will not affect the entire portfolio in the same way.

asset allocation
an expanded version of diversification, in which capital is invested in different markets, such as stocks, bonds, and real estate. The purpose in allocation is to avoid a negative impact on the entire portfolio if and when a particular market suffers a downturn.

5. *Investment time risk.* Most people acknowledge the fact that, were it possible to hold on to real estate long enough, it would eventually become profitable. The *time risk* in real estate involves cash flow because you need to generate income adequate to cover all of the expenses and payments required by owning real estate—and

> **Key Point**
>
> Time often determines success or failure in real estate investing. Profits are secondary. If you need to hold on to real estate longer than you want, that destroys your annualized return and ties up capital.

time risk
the risk in real estate that profits will not materialize in the desired time frame. In that case, investors either accept losses or convert properties to longer-term rentals.

over a lengthy period of time in some cases. Property flipping is designed to generate a profit in a very short period; but the risk is that profit will not be possible in that time. This means you either have to get rid of the property and accept a loss or convert it to a long-term hold. With this in mind, the risk can be mitigated in the selection of property. The potential for fast profit is a key to the property flipping strategy. In addition, however, it may be necessary to also investigate the rental market and to compare market rents to the level of payments a property would require as a long-term hold. Because this additional criterion would limit the potential market for property flipping, it is often ignored or left out of the analytical equation.

Comparisons Between Flipping and Holding

An important step in the analysis of property and the feasibility of a specific strategy requires comparisons. Will it be more profitable to flip properties or to hold for the longer term? To expand this question a little more: Will it be more profitable one way or the other, *and* what are the relative risks?

It is likely that the differences in cash flow between the two strategies will ultimately define those risk levels and compel you to move toward one strategy or the other. More conservative, risk-averse investors tend to want well-priced rental properties, especially if and when the cash flow picture is favorable. Criteria include strong rental demand, affordability of the property itself, current condition (of property and neighborhood), and required down payment. Less conservative investors tend to seek extremely short-term profits through property flipping. The bargain-hunting aspect to property flipping is only one element of this approach. In addition, property flipping involves the ability to identify not only the price advantage, but also to grasp precisely the current market conditions. Property flipping works best at times when demand is very strong and values are growing strongly.

A worthwhile exercise to go through before deciding how to invest in real estate involves comparing flipping and holding. The following are valid means for comparison between these two markets:

1. *Market conditions in your area today.* The starting point in any investment is a critical analysis of the market itself. Stock investors seldom are enthusiastic when markets are volatile and weak; they prefer investing when the market is strong and the mood optimistic. The same rule applies in real estate. What are today's conditions and mood? Remember, real estate markets—unlike stocks—are always local, so national averages or news from other areas is not valid in your regional analysis.

2. *Growth history and potential.* Specific study of local growth in market value of property, as well as potential for continued growth, is the second step in your analysis. Part of this has to involve the time element. If property values have increased 20 percent in the past year, that is far more significant than another area where values have doubled, but that took five years. The rate of growth, coupled with the time involved, define potential for continued growth in the future.

3. *Rental market conditions.* The strength or weakness in rental demand defines the market in some respects. The overall trend in market value is usually associated with owner-occupied, single-family housing. Rental markets, however, may anticipate future trends in the overall market. While owner-occupied housing is an entirely separate market than the market for rental apartment units and houses, the two are related, and demand in one market affects future growth potential in the other. If a previously strong rental demand is beginning to weaken due to overbuilding of apartments, that means that rental houses may be going up for sale in the near future. And with more inventory on the market, that may also mean a slowdown in the rate of growth in housing market values.

   This example is simplistic, of course, because many factors come into play in setting real estate values. However, it does illustrate one way that rental demand—increasing or decreasing—will affect property values in the future.

4. *Interest rate trends.* More than any other single economic feature, interest rates have an immediate effect on property values. With historically low rates from 2000 to 2005, real estate values in many regions continued to grow at double-digit rates. In part, this was caused by higher demand as more people were able to qualify for homes—because their payments were lower with reduced interest rates, meaning a broader qualification for conventional financing. Strong demand is always going to be a feature directly tied to low interest rates; and by the same argument, as interest and mortgage rates begin rising, demand for real estate slows down as well. Although other regional factors definitely affect real estate, interest rates cannot be ignored. With high rates, housing demand may not change due to local factors such as a growing population (related to employment opportunities, for example), so two or more economic realities may offset one another.

5. *Your personal financial condition and risk tolerance.* Finally, any investment comparison has to rest with personal factors. You need to be comfortable with a strategy and the market involved before you proceed, or the decision will not be a good one. In the case of real estate, some people are naturally conservative and will seek the safest possible long-term situation; others are willing to take greater risks in exchange for higher short-term profits, and will pursue property flipping strategies (assuming that market conditions are appropriate). To a great extent, your risk tolerance is determined by your personal financial condition: income, investment capital, and net worth. You need to be able to afford the strategy, and by definition you are only able to tolerate what you can afford, what you understand, and what represents a good fit with your circumstances, conditions, experience, and investing goals.

risk tolerance
the level of risk you are able to accept in a particular product or market, determined by personal income and net worth; experience; and investing goals, attitudes, and preferences.

Key Point

It is a mistake to enter a market based solely on generalized advice. Your personal circumstances should dictate what risks you can afford to take and, as a result, how and where to invest.

Defining your level of investment risk and potential—in terms of what you want and what you can afford—is always an essential part of the investment process. This also includes defining your entrance and exist strategy, whether in the stock market or in real estate. You need to set goals and contingency plans so that you know in advance what you need to do as market conditions change. The next chapter examines this topic.

Getting In, Getting Out

Defining Your Entrance and Exit Strategies

Every investor discovers—one way or the other—that a sharp definition is the key to success. If you define your entrance and exit strategies, then you create a road map for the timing of decisions, identification of profits, and prevention of loss.

Without these three elements, no investment is likely to succeed. Just as business budgets and forecasts are used to identify spending limits and revenue goals, the investment plan requires advance planning and definition. In the financial world, a popular saying is, "If you don't know where you're going, any road will get you there." This is the whole point. In real estate, definition is just as important as it is in the stock market. In property flipping, definition ensures that you identify risk and opportunity levels and that you know not only when to buy but when to sell. The following expands on this concept:

1. *Timing of decisions.* Every investment's success is based on *when* you buy and *when* you sell. Because prices change continuously, poor timing means a potential profit will come out as a loss, or that greater profits will be lost. So timing of decisions requires in-depth knowledge of your local real estate market. By knowing where the property flipping opportunities are to be found, you can maximize the timing of your decision to buy and your decision to sell.

Key Point

Real estate success is not limited to price. It depends on the timing of purchase and sale.

---

2. *Identification of profits.* A second aspect to any form of investing or speculating in real estate is found in the identification of prof-

annualized return

the comparative profit from an investment expressed as if the holding period were exactly one year.

its. This means setting a profit goal for yourself. Some investors want to double their money, whereas others are happy with netting out 20 percent per year. Profits have to be carefully defined by combining yield and time. A 10 percent profit earned over one month is far greater than a 20 percent profit that takes 12 months to earn. When these two outcomes are expressed as the *annualized return*, you find that a shorter holding period often translates to a far greater net profit.

To calculate annualized return, divide the yield by the number of months in the holding period, and then multiply by 12. This calculation is based on the use of months; it can also be performed using weeks or days. If you use weeks, divide the yield by the number of weeks and then multiply by 52. If you use days, divide the yield by the number of days and then multiply by 365. These various methods are summarized in Table 2.1.

For example, a property was owned for 35 days and the profit upon sale was 5 percent. Yield can be calculated using any of the three methods:

Months:	.05	÷	1.17	×	12	= 51.3%
Weeks:	.05	÷	5	×	52	= 52.0%
Days:	.05	÷	35	×	365	= 52.1%

Key Point

Setting profit goals is essential if you hope to measure and quantify your success in real estate investing.

TABLE 2.1	Calculating Annualized Return	
Calculation Method	*Multiplier*	*Formula[a]*
Months	12	$(Y \div H) \times 12$
Weeks	52	$(Y \div H) \times 52$
Days	365	$(Y \div H) \times 365$

[a]Y = yield
H = holding period

The three methods vary slightly, but as long as you use one method consistently, the outcome for various properties will be useful. This *comparative analysis* is an important and valuable tool for every investor. It is used to compare yield on different investments, or to calculate potential yield before the investment has even been made.

comparative analysis
a technique in which two or more investments are compared using the same basic assumptions such as annualized yield. This is used in comparing final outcomes and for judging investment potential in advance.

3. *Prevention of loss.* Most investors focus on profit potential when entering an investment program. However, it is equally important to be aware of the possibility of loss. As part of your risk analysis, be aware of the potential losses as well as profits, and identify methods for reducing and preventing loss. While you cannot ensure 100 percent loss prevention, you can identify by way of exit strategies when you will cut your losses. You may establish the maximum loss you will accept, at which point you will sell. You can also predetermine a maximum holding period with the idea that you will sell by that time. In this case, you limit both the potential profit *and* the potential loss in the event property values fall.

Key Point

Emphasis and focus is usually placed on profit potential. Equally important is a strategic plan to anticipate and reduce potential losses as well.

Definition as a Starting Point in All Investing

The very idea that an investment strategy should be planned and defined in advance simply makes good sense. Even so, this concept is often not put into action. This is unfortunate because, for many reasons, those property flipping strategies that have been carefully defined in advance are more likely to succeed than those that have been poorly planned or not planned at all.

Property flipping as a strategy (like all forms of investing) can and should be defined in advance. This ensures that you comprehend and appreciate the risks involved (as well as the profit potential); that it fits appropriately into your financial plan and broader investment portfolio; and is used properly to achieve your personal goals.

Definition contains several aspects, which can be defined by asking a series of questions:

fixer-upper

a property purchased primarily to upgrade through repairs, with the idea of spending minimum cash on cosmetic changes and then selling for a profit.

1. *What is your specific definition of property flipping?* Not everyone agrees on the definition of the property flipping strategy. Some view it as a purely speculative move and want to take advantage of strong, growing markets without any desire to hold equity positions. Others see flipping as a way to go in and out of equity positions, leaving open the possibility of holding some properties over time, treating other properties as *fixer-upper* properties, and becoming involved with raw land, residential, commercial, industrial, and lodging properties.

2. *What is your short-term goal involving property flipping?* Just as your definition of property flipping may vary from what others believe, you may further define your strategy in terms of what you want to achieve in the next three to six months. Do you have a specific percentage of net profit in mind, and how do you define "profit?" Some think primarily of their cash investment and the net cash received upon sale, and consider the difference as profit. Others concentrate on market value and calculate profit based on purchase price versus sales price.

Calculating *cash-based profit* involves dividing the difference by the initial investment. For example, if you purchase a property with $10,000 and two months later sell and receive a net of $12,000 after expenses, your cash-based profit is 20 percent in one month (or 120 percent annualized):

cash-based profit
a calculation of profit from property flipping based solely on a comparison between cash invested upon purchase and cash received upon sale.

$$(\$12,000 - \$10,000) \div \$10,000$$
$$= 20\% \text{ (two months)}$$

$$(20\% \div 2) \times 12 = 120\% \text{ (annualized)}$$

Calculating *net profit* based on changes in market value is a more traditional approach. The difference between net sales price and original net purchase price is divided by the original net purchase price. For example, if you purchased a property for and adjusted price of $135,000 and sold it two months later for an adjusted price of $155,000, your net profit was:

net profit
the calculated profit based on a comparison between adjusted sales price and adjusted purchase price. The difference between the two is divided by the adjusted purchase price and expressed as a percentage.

$$(\$155,000 - \$135,000) \div \$135,000 = 14.8\% \text{ (two months)}$$

$$(14.8\% \div 2) \times 12 = 88.8\% \text{ (annualized)}$$

Setting goals for short-term profit—on the basis of cash flow or net profit—is one way you define your short-term goals for property flipping. The standard you set compared to actual outcomes also helps you to recognize how realistic your goals were at the time they were set, and helps you to adjust your goals to reflect realities in the market.

Key Point
In calculating profit, cash flow is often far more important than pure profit or loss. If you can't afford to keep the property, *potential* by itself is of no value.

3. *How do you anticipate flipping in your long-term plan?* The short-term plan is useful when you intend to move in and out of positions as quickly as possible. This is the popular view of flipping; it involves not only creating a profit, but doing so as rapidly as possible. In practice, however, there are many reasons why you may end up holding property longer than you originally planned.

Market conditions can change unexpectedly, making a planned property flip less desirable than it appeared. As a result, you may have a choice of selling at a loss or holding on to the property and waiting out the market. A sensible backup position in this situation is to convert the flip property to a rental, to cover your ongoing costs (mortgage payments, insurance, and taxes). You may also change your mind if you see that the market is continuing to grow strongly, and decide to hold the property even though a profit would be immediately possible.

So your long-term plans have to remain flexible due to the possibility of a changing market, as well as your own perceptions about current and future value. Investors often enter positions with one set of assumptions, only to find them changed later.

4. *What risk levels are appropriate for you today, and what factors will change these risk levels in the future?* The key to any investment's success is based on risk—the market risk and cash flow risk associated with real estate. More to the point, the match between risk and suitability defines how appropriate real estate is for you. In order for property flipping to be an appropriate strategy, you need to ensure that you have adequate cash income and resources available to cover all contingencies. You also need to understand the local market for real estate and how its trend has been moving in recent months. Finally, you will need strong credit in order to finance the flipping strategy.

Your acceptable risk level will evolve in the future as your own circumstances change. Major events (marriage, purchasing a home, birth of a child, changes in job or career, divorce, death of a family member) all change your risk level. Changes in your annual income (from advancement in your career, inheritance, or ill health) also change your risk level. No one's risk level remains the same forever. Even while other circumstances remain the same, as your personal investing experience evolves, that also will affect how you view risk and what types of risk become important to you. If you have a lot of liquid investments (in savings, stocks, and mutual funds), you will be better able to manage directly owned real estate. So virtually all change—in your circumstances, status, job, health, and experience—also changes your risk level. What you consider appropriate today is likely to be outdated in a year or two.

5. *Do you have a time frame in mind for this strategy?* In planning any investment strategy, everyone can benefit by applying the tried-and-true business models used by the most successful corporations. Time frame—how long will it take to accomplish the goal?—is the means by which you define *when* and *how* you will accomplish your property flipping objectives. Just based on the calculation of return on your money, it is clearly a greater advantage to earn 10 percent in two months than in two years. The two-month timing model translates to an annualized 60 percent return, whereas the two-year model is only a 5 percent annualized return.

There is more to the time frame than just the rate of return. The longer it takes for you to realize your specific goals in a property flipping strategy, the longer your money is tied up. This does not only mean your capital is idle; it also means you have to pay interest to a lender, manage cash flow, and spend money on insurance, property taxes, and maintenance. So the time frame is more than a calculation—it is the study of the time you require to achieve your goals, given the cost of keeping property. Therefore, your cost for a two-month turnaround will not only be more profitable, it will also produce greater overall return because you won't have to give part of your profits to lenders, local tax collectors, and insurance companies.

6. *What is your ideal financial gain from the activity?* The preceding sections introduced several important considerations in defining exactly what you expect to accomplish in your property flipping program. Given the constraints of the market and the potential for sudden change in price direction, it makes sense to decide up front what your ideal financial gain should be. At the same time, you should also identify a bailout point. Just as stock market investors often use a trailing stop to capture paper gains and minimize losses, real estate investors can do the same thing by setting goals.

For example, you might define your financial outcome as "a 20 percent net return within three months or less." You may further decide that "if the price of the property has not risen by 20 percent or more within three months, it should be listed and resold." This decision limits your exposure to ongoing expenses and, while it may translate to a net loss on the investment, it might be better than holding for many more months and suffering even larger losses. If the market has gone soft, it makes no sense to accumulate interest and other expenses hoping that prices may turn strong again soon.

Another example involves a decision to revert from property flipping to a hold-and-rent strategy. For example, your goal might be stated as "a 20 percent net return within three months or less" and, in addition, "if the price of the property has not risen by 20 percent or more within three months, it will be rented out."

The goal should include this contingency plan as a way of anticipating the worst-case situation. If the price market goes soft, that does not mean the rental market will be soft as well. If you purchased the property at a bargain price, it might be possible to achieve very strong positive cash flow by renting it out. This gives you time to wait out the market until demand grows strong again.

Entry Strategies and Examples

An *entry strategy* in any investment involves deciding on the type of property or product, the price, location, and ideal holding period. In the case of buying stocks, you need to determine (1) the type of investment (directly owned stock or shares of a mutual fund); (2) the price (price per share); (3) location (industry sector or country); and (4) ideal holding period (speculation based on short-term price movement or long-term growth stock). The same criteria apply to real estate as well.

entry strategy
the identification of type, price, location, and holding period that will be employed in property flipping or in any type of invest-

The list can be fine-tuned even more and, in fact, a fifth element has to be added: Whether you plan to move in and out of the property or perform repairs and take more time. This and similar actions are termed *strategic decisions*—which, along with the other criteria, are described in more detail:

1. *Type of property.* While the emphasis for most people will be on single-family residential property, a wide range of other choices is possible. For example, you might want to speculate in raw land, multifamily housing (duplexes, triplexes, or small apartment buildings), or commercial or industrial property. Because part of your overall selection will involve becoming familiar with your local real estate market, a sensible place to start is by deciding what type of property you will include.

2. *Price.* Virtually everyone is limited by the price of property. Few people can afford to start out buying an industrial park or a large apartment building. Price limits what you can do, but the potential price range may be considerable. Price is not limited to the stated sales price of property; in a very real sense, it involves two far more important considerations: how much financing you can obtain and what level of cash flow is likely to occur.

   Financing actually determines what you can afford more than price. If you are told by a lender that you need a 20 percent down payment and you have only $20,000, your investment range will be limited to $100,000 or less. Exceptions apply—for example—when you can obtain additional financing or a seller is willing to carry a loan, your financing limitations will be raised.

   Cash flow—the comparison between income from investments and expenses and payments—will determine whether you can afford a specific property. In some markets, cash flow problems are very restrictive. In Manhattan and San Francisco, for example, property values are so high that cash flow won't work out unless you are able to produce a substantial down payment. In other areas, property values are far lower but rental rates are high enough to produce workable cash flow levels.

3. *Location.* All real estate value is ultimately determined by location. This is more than a reference to regions of the country, however. All real estate value and the supply and demand that drives the market is extremely local in nature. So you cannot rely on national averages or even regional averages; you need to study the market in the city or town where you plan to invest. Even in one community, value varies from one neighborhood to another, often substantially. Location within a single market defines the rest of your entry strategy.

> ### Key Point
>
> How long do you intend to hold a property? The answer defines the types of strategies you will need to employ.

4. *Ideal holding period.* The property flipping strategy often involves a quick turnaround in the holding period. But based on the strength of the local market, the type of property, and your specific investment goals, the actual holding period may vary considerably. In some flipping strategies (to be explained later in the book), a property can be sold even before it has been bought, using options. In other strategies, you might decide to hold a property for months or even years before selling it.

5. *Strategic decisions.* The actual holding period determines how you manage a property while you own it. While some people move in and out of properties rapidly (at times in a matter of days), others hold and flip properties over a longer period of time. You might decide to specialize in rundown properties needing only cosmetic repairs—going on the theory that investing only a few dollars will dramatically increase property values. You might see an opportunity in a market with weak prices but strong rental demand, meaning you can create positive cash flow while waiting out the supply-and-demand market. You can also decide to convert a property from the original purpose of flipping it to use as your primary residence. Many variations in strategic decisions are possible, dictated by changing market conditions.

The Ideal Holding Period

The purpose in detailed and exhaustive definition—before purchasing property—is to ensure that you have focused on the most appropriate and narrow market. Matching markets to your budget, objectives, and risk tolerance level ensures that you will not unintentionally buy properties outside of the desired range.

The degree of market research and definition you perform in advance will also lead to a higher rate of success in selecting the best properties based on what you hope to accomplish. Even so, many investors

---

Key Point

Matching markets to your personal risks and goals is the best way to avoid buying the wrong property. This is not a big secret—nevertheless, many people forget this in their approach to investing.

---

have difficulty identifying the ideal holding period. When viewed in advance, it is not always possible to know the conditions of the market once the purchase has closed; and based on how the market changes, your ideal holding period may need to be flexible.

The holding period will be defined by what you plan to do with the property. Are there repairs to perform? Are you going to rent out the property and, if so, on a month-to-month basis or through a lease? These questions also affect how and when you sell. Although occupancy by a tenant may continue even as you market and sell your property, a long-term lease limits the potential market of buyers. Some buyers will not want to acquire the obligations of a lease as they will have other ideas about buying property, such as living in it themselves.

If repairs are going to be performed as part of an extremely short-term ownership period, it might be possible to negotiate completion of minor repairs during escrow. It is not practical for you to spend money on repairs before close—and you might be prohibited from doing so. If you know the cost in advance, you can arrange for completion of those repairs such as when your property is negotiated to close at $150,000 and you know that $15,000 in repairs will have to be performed. You may provide the cash within escrow and allow the seller to complete those repairs before the closing date. This is risky because if the deal falls through, how will you get your money back? The deposit would have to be refundable, which also complicates the deal. It is one of many possible ways to speed up the process, but it is not always a wise move.

Another alternative is to line up and schedule work to be performed immediately after the close of the deal. Contractors line up work for weeks in advance during the busy months, so if you need a contractor's participation, make the appointment as early as you can. This ensures that you will not have to wait for weeks until the contractor can perform the repairs for you.

Having work lined up to be completed as quickly as possible is also sensible if you plan to keep the property as a rental. If you plan to move someone in after repairs have been completed, you need to line up workers as early as possible, well before the close of escrow. The longer you have to wait after the close, the longer the property will remain unoccupied. It is not practical to try and complete work on the inside of the house *after* a tenant has moved in. This is not fair to the tenant and will only cause trouble. If work is needed on the inside, it should be completed before you even advertise the property. This avoids disruption and will also draw a higher market rent. If a house is in disrepair, potential tenants will not be willing to pay full market rent, even if you intend to fix current problems. Repairs have to be completed before you begin interviewing tenants.

The amount of work you are going to perform on the property—and the cost of that work—will often define how long your holding period has to be. In a clean in-and-out property flip, you buy and sell quickly without spending any additional funds. This works in situations where property does not need repairs; but if you do plan to perform repairs, the time required also determines how long you need to hold the property.

A strictly cosmetic repair situation can be a short-term hold. If you simply need to clean up the landscaping, repair a fence, and paint the outside of the house, all of that work can be done in a week or less (assuming you have the people lined up to get right to it). But if you also need to paint all of the inside rooms, put on a new roof, and fix or replace floors, appliances, and the heater, it is likely that you will need to allow for more time, perhaps a month or more, before you can plan to list and sell the property. The level of repairs often defines how long you have to wait before you can sell. If your yard cleanup is the only work you plan to do, one or two days is all you will need; but for repairs beyond the merely cosmetic, the schedule will be dictated by the complexity of the work, availability of contractors, and the degree to which several repairs can be completed concurrently. If you need to paint the whole exterior *and* replace all of the carpeting, it will make more sense to

---

Key Point

If you will need to complete repairs, it will often determine how long you will need to hold the property. Be sure you know how long a list of repairs is going to take before deciding on a holding period.

complete the painting first. Trying to install new carpeting at the same time that painters are on site is not practical.

Scheduling work can be problematic as well. Let's say your painter tells you the whole inside can be painted in two days; is it safe to schedule delivery of carpets for the third day? What if the painting takes four days instead of two? You need to ensure that estimates of time required are realistic and that you allow for problems. You will be better off allowing some flexibility in your schedule and getting everything done, so that your planned schedule will not end up with excessive delays.

Your Role in Managing the Investment

The method you choose for investing in real estate will also define your own role. Unlike the stock market, in which your role is limited to buying and selling, real estate requires more direct decisions. If you simply move in and out of positions and focus on short-term flipping strategies, your role will probably be very limited. You will deal with escrow agents or attorneys, contractors, lenders, appraisers, and a few other experts; but you will not necessarily need to be involved directly in managing the property.

This all changes if you decide to hold on to the property and create cash flow through rental income. In this case you need to take tenant applications, check out background and credit, complete a rental agreement, and then collect rent each month. As a landlord, you are also responsible for repairs and maintenance, and you need to balance rental income against ongoing mortgage payments, utilities, insurance, property taxes, and the cost of repairs.

Many people want to emphasize the speculative nature of property flipping and avoid the entire landlord-and-tenant relationship. While it can be lucrative, it involves risks on many levels and can be time consuming and expensive. Even a relatively short period of vacancy or nonpayment of rent

---

Key Point

You may view property flipping as a clean in-and-out strategy. But even with good planning, it doesn't always work out that way. If you end up holding property longer than anticipated, plan for managing tenants.

drains your personal budget, and unexpected repairs can make the investment an expensive proposition. For these reasons, investors may conclude that the complexities and risks of landlord strategies are not worth the trouble.

One alternative is to hire a professional management company to insulate you from direct contact with tenants. For a fee averaging 10 percent of rents collected, the company deals with tenants in all respects, including screening, collecting rent, and approving on going repairs. For many people, the tax advantages of holding rental property justify the headaches. You can deduct up to $25,000 of net losses every year from real estate held directly (less if your adjusted gross income is higher than $100,000), and using a management company protects you from the potential problems of working directly with tenants. Even when you intend to flip property short term, you can end up managing the property directly and becoming a landlord. This is one of the risks of property flipping; but professional management reduces the risk for a fee.

As with all investments, there are arguments pro and con about degrees of personal involvement. These often determine the overall viability of a specific strategy as a primary reason for making the decision (with other reasons including affordability, market risk, and cash flow). More than with most types of risk, your comfort level with a particular strategy should be among the most important considerations. Just as those trading on the stock market can be uncomfortable with some strategies due to risk exposure, real estate investors need to make informed comparisons. Your beginning analysis should include a three-part test:

1. *What do you know about a particular strategy?* Knowledge may offset a perception that a strategy is exotic or high risk. The more knowledge you acquire, the more informed you are about the strategy. You might find out that the real range of risks is not uncomfortable—or that there are many more risks than you thought. The key is to find out all you can about how the idea actually works.

Key Point

Always invest using the three-part test: What do you know, are you aware of risks, and what are your choices?

2. *Are you comfortable with the risks involved?* Once you learn all about real estate strategies, you will also know about the many types of risk involved. Many people focus only on profit potential and ignore the very real risks, and there are many types. Chapter 1 explained and compared these various types of risk. The key point to be made here is that, in terms of your personal role in managing your real estate investments, are you comfortable with the risks? If you are, then you're well equipped to proceed. If you are not, then you are well advised to look for alternatives.

3. *What are the alternatives?* There are always alternatives to investing money in one particular way. The most obvious is to *not* invest, but to look elsewhere. You can also find more conservative ways to invest in real estate, including buying shares of a real estate investment trust (REIT) or a real estate-oriented exchange-traded fund, mortgage pool, or limited partnership. You can also put off a decision until you have more income and investment capital, or until current market conditions are more favorable. Finally, if you do decide to proceed with property flipping, be sure you research the market completely, and if you end up having to work with tenants, consider hiring a professional management company to insulate yourself from direct contact with tenants.

Postentry Strategies

Once your role in managing your investments has been defined, the next step is to determine your postentry strategies. If you intend to simply buy and sell properties with as short a holding period as possible, that is one approach and, in a sense, it is also a postentry strategy. You may decide that your exact goal is to have as short a holding period as possible, and to spend as little extra cash as possible before you close a sale.

Key Point

Postentry strategies are a form of budgeting—of money, time, and investment resources.

For any other variation on property flipping, you will need to develop postentry strategies in four major areas. These are:

1. *Improvements.* If your property is going to work as a fixer-upper, you will need to ensure that you buy properties with the appropriate level of needed repairs. For example, if you have a limited cash budget and you intend to perform only cosmetic repairs, you will need a home inspection before closing to ensure that the property does not also need major (and expensive) repairs. The seller should be required as a condition of sale to pay for and complete those major repairs before closing.

   In developing a list of improvements to perform, keep an eye on the cost as well. If you want to resell in the short term, you will want to keep improvement costs to as small a number as possible. Even necessary repairs do not always reflect higher market value within the first year or two after they are completed. So you need to prepare a detailed list of needed improvements and how much they will cost, and make sure that you will be able to sell the property with enough profit to justify this effort.

2. *Financing and refinancing.* Few investors keep property indefinitely without refinancing. Even if you hold property for only a short period of time, financing terms often determine your real profit or loss. Interest rate and loan origination fees can add thousands of dollars to your true net cost for acquiring property, not to mention the drain on cash over a few months' time. Shopping for the best loan deal makes a big difference in what you pay for property, including the difference in rates between adjustable- and fixed-rate mortgages. If you plan to hold on to property less than one or two years, seek a competitively priced, adjustable-rate loan. This will save you thousands over the holding period.

   If you later decide to convert the property to a rental and keep it for more than your original target time, you may also want to refinance the original mortgage to find a more attractive permanent rate, or a more attractive rate based on current market conditions and interest rate trends.

3. *Renting policies.* If and when your property flipping strategy converts to a longer-term rental, you face decisions concerning your policies as a landlord. In anticipation of this possibility, examine the local market and interview property managers. If you decide

to hire a management company, you need to know ahead of time which ones have solid reputations and experience and are willing to work with you, what their fees are, and whether their location is going to be a good match for your properties. You also need to determine market rents and look at the conditions of the market (vacancy rates, numbers of units existing and under construction, longer-term trends in the rental market). You also need to locate forms for rental application and rental agreement, and an inventory of conditions you will need in working with tenants. A professional management company can supply the proper forms as well as fill the job of advertising, interviewing tenants, checking backgrounds, and collecting security deposits and rent. If you decide to manage properties directly, you need to find the forms and spend time on these other steps yourself.

4. *Additional leverage.* If you end up holding property for longer than a month or two, you may want to refinance the original loan. In doing so, it might also be possible to get cash out, especially if you bought the property at a price below current market value. An appraisal may reveal that you have more equity in the property, which can be used as additional leverage. Upon refinancing, it is possible to use the extra cash as a down payment on a second property flip.

Exit Strategies and Examples

Your exit strategies will not always match your entry strategies. While this relatively simple idea seems obvious, it is, in fact, a profound reality concerning all investing.

Exit strategies are *not* driven by preentry assumptions. In fact, the means by which you exit an investment will be determined by what actually occurs after your purchase. Exit strategies may be designed to cut losses, to adjust timing based on a changed market, or to figure out how to sell a property with problems (which you did not know in

Key Point
Exit strategies are usually adjustments to your previous plan, based on unanticipated circumstances in market value, conditions, and costs.

advance) such as structural flaws. These strategies may also be aimed at determining exactly when and why you will sell a property. These strategies may involve reaching specific goals or may involve combining multiple properties into a single sale. Exit strategies include:

1. *Identifying and reaching profit goals.* Your original plan may have identified a desired profit level. You might have set the goal for yourself to sell the flipped property for a net cash profit of 20 percent (20 percent increase on actual cash invested) or a 20 percent increase in market value (selling the property at an adjusted sales price 20 percent above the adjusted purchase price). However, market conditions may have changed since you closed on the property. If the market has softened and you anticipate further decline in prices (or reduction in the rate of growth), it may be wise to sell now and accept a lower profit. If the market has heated up, you may decide to hold the property longer than originally planned to create greater potential profits.

2. *Identifying and reaching time goals.* The goals you set might not be limited to profits. You might be more interested in getting in and out of a deal in a specific time frame, such as two months or six months. Because conditions may have changed since buying the property, however, you will not always have control over the time element. It might be necessary to sell sooner than planned or to wait longer than you thought. It might also become attractive to convert the flipped property to a long-term hold and rent it out. Because you cannot know how conditions are going to change, it is wise to remain flexible and be willing to change your exit strategy based on market conditions.

3. *Locating the right buyer.* When real estate markets tighten up—meaning there are more sellers than buyers—it is not always possible to find the "right" buyer. This may be defined as a buyer who can qualify for financing, is willing to make an offer at the level you need to achieve, or is even serious. In slow markets, bargain hunters seek opportunities and may offer deep discounts, seeking the desperate seller. To locate the right buyer in a slowed-down market, you might have to be patient, offer incentives (such as paying the buyer's closing costs, including a carpet allowance, or providing free appliances, for example), or pay a broker a full commission in exchange for an extra marketing push.

4. *Bundling several properties together.* Some real estate investors purchase a number of properties, raw land, or abandoned buildings (often through foreclosure sales) with the idea of bundling them together in a single sale. These *bundled lots* may include any number of properties in various conditions. The appeal of bundling is that the collective properties are discounted due to volume. If done with good property flipping discretion, you can make a profit by bundling properties and still offer a discount to a buyer (another speculator, a contractor, or a developer, for example).

bundled lots

several properties acquired at discount and offered for sale in a single transaction.

5. *Marketing a problem property.* You might end up with a property that has special problems. It may be a *nonconforming property*, meaning it is not similar to other properties in the same area. A property with an exceptionally large lot, more than the average number of rooms, or unusual design is going to be difficult to market, and is not likely to attract more value than the average conforming property in the area. In this situation, you should be aware of the nonconformity problem when you buy and anticipate problems upon offering the property for sale.

6. *Writing an escape clause into the contract.* Many real estate contracts include one or more *contingencies*, conditions that must be met in order for the contract to be binding. For example, a financing contingency accepts a buyer's offer, but only if financing is approved by a specific date. If that does not occur, the deal falls through. Other contingencies deal with the sale of another property or the outcome of inspections, completion of specific repairs, or changes in current zoning of the property. As a buyer, you can provide yourself with an escape clause in the form of a contingency, allowing you to back out of a deal if you discover flaws in the property. The typical "contingent upon inspection" clause allows you to demand that a seller perform repairs as part of the contract. You can also provide yourself a way out by the wording of the financing contingency—such as making the deal contingent on obtaining financing

nonconforming property

any property whose features are dissimilar to other properties in the same area, including lot size, condition, number of rooms, overall square feet, or design. Market appreciation of nonconforming properties is inhibited by their dissimilar features or attributes.

well below current market rates. This way, you can exercise a cancellation of the deal if you wish.

Contingencies should not be used to negotiate in bad faith; but thinking ahead to the possibility that you might change your mind before the deal closes and need the exit strategy, it does not hurt to give yourself the bargaining power and a way to get out of the deal if you need to.

A summary of the preentry, entry, postentry and exit strategies and considerations is shown in Figure 2.1.

The next chapter examines the various roles you play in property flipping and ways to participate in the market, and explains the role of the many professional individuals and companies you will need in order to succeed as a real estate investor.

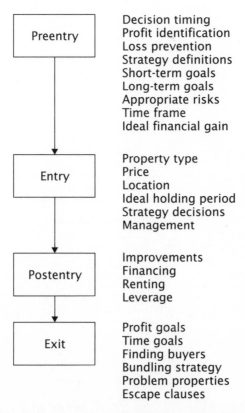

FIGURE 2.1 Preentry, Entry, Postentry and Exit Strategies

The Cast of Players
Scouts, Dealers, Retailers, and More

A "cast of characters" is needed to properly execute a complete real estate transaction. In fact, many different experts get involved in the process of buying and selling property. Compared to buying or selling stocks, you might use a broker and a research service at the most. Some investors even do it all themselves, running their entire portfolio without any outside help and trading online from the comfort of home. This is not possible in real estate.

The property flipping transaction is no different from other strategies, with the exception that it often takes place in a relatively short period of time. Most of the resources needed to complete this transaction are present even in the fastest transaction, including investors, who participate in property flipping in many different roles—as scouts, dealers, or retailers.

The Property Scout

The *scout* may be thought of as a market researcher. The scout's function is to investigate the market, locate property flipping opportunities, and to advise other investors about those opportunities.

> **scout**
> an individual who researches the market to locate property flipping opportunities, and then reports those opportunities to other investors.

Key Point

A scout does the groundwork for others and is paid for the value of research. A talented scout knows where all the goods deals are.

A scout, of course, works for another real estate professional, often a broker or agent, or a speculator with a lot of money; so the scout is usually a good place to start out as a novice. By doing the groundwork, you're getting an education while earning money, and the scout's function is the best place for the novice. Once you become more experienced in your own right, you may want to hire and use a scout to help you find properties to trade on your own.

Why would you want to operate as a scout? The function simply performs a service, either for an up-front fee or for a portion of the profits. In that respect, the scout acts as an agent for someone else. You might want to work as a scout for a number of reasons:

1. *The risks are far lower.* The scout invests only time, and may be paid for the effort even if nothing comes from it. Compensation is a matter negotiated between the scout and the equity investor or speculator. Even if the investor loses money, the scout is often paid when information is provided. In a more entrepreneurial arrangement, the scout agrees with a dealer or retailer to take part in a share of the profits. But this is a less certain approach. The money might be better if and when a deal is made—and if it is profitable. Under the shared profit arrangement, there is no guarantee that the scout will be paid at all.

   Some real estate agents work as scouts by looking for properties on behalf of clients, especially if those clients are out of town. The idea is that the client will eventually purchase a property and the agent will then earn a commission. However, there is no assurance that a deal will ever be made, or that the client will hire the agent. When anyone acts as a scout without being paid up front, there is always a chance that they will not be paid at all.

2. *You might not have the capital to buy real estate yourself.* Many people would invest in real estate if only they had the money. For them, the role of scout may be a promising path to becoming an investor. If you act as a scout for someone else, you are paid for your efforts. A finder's fee is all a matter of what you can negoti-

ate with the principal. Some scouts also work for a share of the eventual profits or, if the scout is also a real estate agent, for a cut of the commissions. At the same time, you learn all about local real estate, which will invariably be valuable for you later on. The more you know about local conditions, the better positioned you are to make a profit from property flipping.

3. *Some people are better suited to research than to taking risks.* Not everyone is suited temperamentally to property flipping, at least not as a direct participant. There are certainly risks involved; and if you prefer the research phase of the real estate transaction, acting as a scout may be a perfect solution.

4. *This is a great way to gain experience.* If you are not completely familiar with real estate in your area (analyzing and valuing properties, finding bargains, and learning the subtle differences between neighborhoods, for example) you can think of being a scout as the best place to learn the ropes.

The scout's role is summarized in Figure 3.1.

Scouts provide an array of information about the market in general, as well as about a specific neighborhood or even one property. A starting point might be to report on overall local conditions: the current supply of property compared to average closed sales; the spread between asked and sales prices; and time on the market. In other words, the scout may pre-

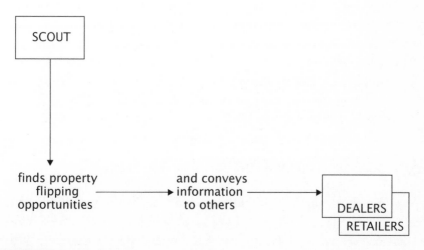

FIGURE 3.1 The Scout

Key Point
The scout is not just an expert in a general sense. He or she also needs to have extensive knowledge of the local market, neighborhoods, and individual properties.

pare a market study for a dealer or retailer, which is a study of the supply-and-demand features of the market today *and* of the trend under way.

A more detailed analysis might involve a comparative study of neighborhoods or areas within a city, town, or county. This is valuable information for anyone not familiar with the market, because it takes time to understand the often subtle differences that may be found in market valuation between properties only a few blocks apart.

Scouts can also find specific properties that meet an investor's criteria: price, location, condition, and an examination of comparable sales in the same neighborhood. Once a dealer or retailer becomes interested in a property, the scout may also investigate further, including checking on the condition of the property, price flexibility, and the reason the house is being sold. The scout's challenge is to find this information simply by asking questions, and not necessarily by checking the obvious sources. The scout can interview the real estate agent holding a listing and even speak with the owner, tenants in rentals, and neighbors to gather this information.

This brings up a second reason that scouts should be paid in advance. If a scout is going to get a share of the profits, there is no incentive to provide negative information about a property. But a scout who is paid for gathering information is free to give the dealer or retailer all of the information about a property. The most valuable information may be negative, giving someone else a reason *not* to buy. So everyone in the transaction will benefit if the scout is free to examine and report both positive and negative facts.

The Real Estate Dealer

The scout works for and provides information to others, including the *dealer* in real estate. A dealer is a real estate wholesaler and often provides go-between services in the capacity of real estate agents or brokers. When a dealer is also licensed to sell real estate, his or her compensation is

> ### Key Point
>
> Think of the dealer as a wholesaler. A talented dealer can find bargains, enabling everyone to make a profit on the deal.

earned through real estate commissions. Dealers may also act separately, and are compensated by marking up properties between their purchase price and the price at which they sell to retailers.

dealer
an individual who buys real estate at a discount, marks it up, and sells at retail, profiting from the difference; or who act as go-between in the capacity of a licensed real estate agent or broker, compensated by commissions.

The dealer who is also a real estate salesperson may earn a considerable fee by acting as both listing and selling agent. Normally, the final commission is split between brokerage firms (and within firms between the agent and the broker), but when the agent acts as dealer, he or she has more control over the transaction. The transaction of property may even be handled quickly and without being made available to the buying public or to other real estate brokers or agents.

For example, an agent/dealer is approached by someone who wants to sell a property. The agent, using a network of contacts, knows of an interested buyer. The agent makes an offer to the seller and arranges to close the deal, and also makes an offer to the potential buyer at the same time. Because this transaction never becomes a listing, it happens quickly and everyone is satisfied with the speed and conclusion of the deal. In fact, when the agent/dealer makes such an arrangement, the whole two-part transaction (seller-to-dealer and dealer-to-buyer) can be handled in a single escrow and closing. That means a single title search and title insurance policy, transfer and recording of title, and other closing costs. The dealer profits from the markup; the seller gets a fast close; and the buyer purchases a property at an attractive price.

> ### Key Point
>
> The real estate agent who also works as a dealer is well poised to find exceptional bargains for investors. This is a valuable resource for every property flipper.

Agents may also become dealers when lenders anticipate needing to foreclose on a defaulted loan. The lender, not wanting to take title to such properties, contacts the agent and offers the property well below market value, with the motivation of wanting to get the property out of its portfolio as quickly as possible. The agent immediately contacts a retail property flipping investor and offers the property for sale. The whole transactions can take place rapidly even when three people or organizations are involved. As long as the discount is deep enough, both dealer and retailer will be able to make a profit.

The dealer's role is summarized in Figure 3.2.

Retailers and Real Estate Markup

The third major player is the *retailer* who ends up with properties from scouts or dealers, or who simply researches the market directly and

retailer

an investor who purchases property on the open market, privately, or through a dealer, with the idea of flipping at a profit.

buys properties that have been listed for sale. The retailer would normally pay market value for properties, but in property flipping strategies, discounted properties are sought and desired. Without having to work through a scout or dealer to acquire discounts, retail property flippers work with developers or contractors, bid directly in the foreclosure market, or do a lot of legwork in the market, often working directly with sellers rather than through listing and selling agents.

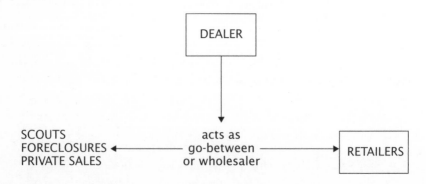

FIGURE 3.2 The Dealer

The retailer typically acquires title to the property and finances the purchase with a down payment and a loan, even when the duration of the holding period is very short. A retailer can move in and out of flipped properties using several different strategies, including:

1. *Options.* The use of options to acquire and sell property is one way to flip without needing a lot of capital. (This is explained in the next chapter.)

2. *Fast close.* When a property flipper lines up a buyer quickly, it is possible to combine the purchase and closing escrow into a single event. This will not always work, but it can be done. When a retailer finds a buyer in this manner, he or she is acting as a quasi-dealer. The difficulty is in finding properties with a deep enough discount to be able to make a profit and still attract a new buyer.

3. *Performing cosmetic improvements in a 30- to 90-day period.* Property flipping can involve performing cosmetic improvements and selling the property as quickly as possible. The cosmetic fixer-upper is often the most lucrative way to flip properties, especially for those who do not have an extensive network of selling and buying contacts.

4. *Longer-term hold and rental.* Finally, a property can be purchased, held as a rental for a few months, and then sold. The demands of cash flow and the risks of working with tenants make this alternative less desirable for those who prefer getting in and out rapidly. But unless you want to hold properties for many years, the short-term equity period with a month-to-month rental agreement is one way to go.

The retailer's role is summarized in Figure 3.3.

FIGURE 3.3   The Retailer

Key Point
A retailer is at a disadvantage compared to the dealer. For this reason, many retailers end up combining those two roles and maximizing their flipping by operating as either a retailer and/or dealer depending on the context of the transaction or the market.

The retailer is less likely able to arrange private deals in which both seller and buyer make a profit. The dealer is better positioned for that strategy; but retailers can develop their network to the point that this becomes possible. Retailers who can link up the selling and buying interests in property often act as both retailers and dealers.

Pinning Down the Costs of Buying and Selling

Perhaps the most difficult task in property flipping is identifying an acceptable profit margin. This is not always simple. Circumstances vary among properties and over time. As prices rise in some areas more rapidly than in the past, investors start to wonder when the bubble will burst. One way to react is to be more cautious and accept lower profits.

Key Point
Real estate investors need to calculate a realistic breakeven point, given the cost of buying and selling, not to mention holding property. This task is not as obvious as it may seem at first.

Every investor faces the dilemma of timing. When should you take profits or cut losses? How do you know when to be in the market or to stay away? What direction will the next trend take?

While these decisions have to be made individually, you can take comfort in what the numbers reveal. That means understanding the specific costs of buying and selling before identifying the level at which you flip your property. In the stock market, trading costs are known in advance. Brokers charge a specific fee or percentage for trading 100 shares of stock, and it is easy to calculate a breakeven point or a profit or loss range. In real estate, the cost of buying and selling is more complex; so your calculations need to take into account the extra costs of going through a purchase or sale transaction.

adjusted purchase price
the stated and agreed-upon price paid for property, plus expenses related to the closing process, financing, and proration of expenses.

The stated purchase price and sales price are always adjusted for a variety of costs. The purchase price is increased by the buyer's closing costs to arrive at the *adjusted purchase price*. These costs include recording and document fees, any fees collected during escrow to pay lender's points and other charges, and any payments buyers have to make for inspections. Finally, certain expenses such as taxes, loan interest, and utilities are subject to *proration* between buyer and seller.

proration
a process of splitting expenses such as taxes, insurance, and utilities between buyer and seller. These expenses are split based on the number of days.

For example, a property tax bill for the period of January 1 through June 30 is due on April 10. The total is $492.15. A purchase closes on March 10. In this 181-day period, the seller is responsible for January 1 through March 10, which is 69 days; and the seller is responsible for the remaining 112 days. The expense is prorated as:

Seller: (69 ÷ 181) × \$492.15 = \$187.62

Buyer: (112 ÷ 181) × \$492.15 = \$304.53

The buyer is responsible for \$304.53, so that amount is prorated at closing, and the bill will be paid through the escrow process. The adjusted purchase price will reflect this added expense.

The *adjusted sales price* is the original and agreed-upon sales price less closing costs. In the example above, the seller's proceeds would be reduced by \$187.62, the prorated portion of the property tax bill. The seller also pays real estate commissions, applicable excise taxes, recording fees, inspection fees, and the cost of repairs negotiated as part of the deal. The level of closing costs varies by the deal and by applicable charges in each state, but you can estimate it fairly closely. If the typical real estate commission (usually the largest part of closing costs) is 6 percent and local excise tax is 1 percent, you can estimate within reason that total closing costs will be at or below 10 percent of the sales price.

The adjustments to both sides of a transaction becomes important when you sell property because the real profit will be based on the adjusted numbers and not just on market value. The adjusted purchase price, also called the *basis* in property in most cases, is subtracted from the adjusted sales price to arrive at the profit. This calculation is summarized in Figure 3.4.

The calculation of *adjusted* purchase and sales prices is the most accurate method for calculating profit or loss from property flipping. Without those adjustments, you could end up losing money even when property values rise. If, for example, you buy property for \$105,000 and its value increases to \$110,000, it appears that a \$5,000 profit has been made. But assuming 2 percent closing costs when you buy and 10 percent closing costs when you sell, the outcome is not as attractive:

adjusted sales price

the negotiated sales price, minus the seller's closing costs including commissions, taxes, recording fees, and inspection fees.

basis

the adjusted purchase price of property or the value used to calculate net gain upon sale. The basis is subtracted from the adjusted sales price to arrive at the true cash-based profit on the sale.

Sales price   _____

Less: seller's closing costs   _____

    Adjusted sales price   _____

Purchase price   _____

Plus: buyer's closing costs   _____

    Adjusted purchase price   _____

    Net profit or loss   _____

FIGURE 3.4   Calculating the Adjusted Purchase Price

Sales price	$110,000
Less: seller's closing costs	−11,000
Adjusted sales price	$99,000
Purchase price	$105,000
Plus: buyer's closing costs	+2,100
Adjusted purchase price	$107,100
Net loss	$8,100

The potential problem of identifying a profit point gets even worse if you spend additional money to repair the property and pay insurance, taxes, and utilities. If you finance the purchase, you also have to pay points and other lender fees and monthly interest. In this example, it will require a much greater gap between adjusted purchase and sales prices to create a profit from property flipping. If you intend to hold on to property for as short a period as possible, creating a net profit needs to occur rapidly, again pointing out how essential it is to get properties at deep discount. The longer you have to wait to get a profit, the higher the

---

Key Point

If you end up holding on to property longer than you planned originally, the ongoing costs and expenses could make it more difficult to
profit from the transaction. Because of this, you need to realistically
plan the numbers *and* the time requirements.

**breakeven
cash flow**
a condition in
which rental in-
come from prop-
erty matches the
sum of all cash
outlays, including
mortgage interest
and principal,
insurance, taxes,
utilities, mainte-
nance, and other
expenses.

interim costs and the greater the difficulty. Even if
you rent out property, rental income is likely to be
offset by the interest, property taxes, insurance, and
utilities costs. And achieving *breakeven cash flow*
will be even more difficult when you hold property
longer than you want.

With the cost element in mind, it is clear that
flipping works only when you can (1) reduce closing costs, (2) work with partners to carry balances,
or (3) achieve deep discounts in the properties you
buy. Closing costs can be reduced if you have a real
estate license and earn at least a portion of the commission; and if you flip only those properties in
which you act as both listing and selling agent, you
cut the commission cost in half. You may also recruit a broker as an
equity partner in order to reduce commission costs even more. The broker may agree to share in profits rather than claiming half of a commission. Other equity partners may include a private lender who will agree
to keep fees down and even waive repayment requirements in exchange
for a share in the equity. (In working with a broker or lender, you combine equity position with the role of dealer.) Finally, the deep discount
opportunity remains the most likely way to create and earn profits from
property flipping. If you pay retail price or close to it, your chances for
selling at a profit in the short term will be slim.

Real Estate Agents and Brokers

You will probably work with a real estate agent to locate and purchase
properties, and again to place the same properties on the market. If you
acquire a real estate license, you can cut a lot of cost out of the transaction and work for your own account (acting as a dealer, for example).

If you can locate a broker who is willing to forgo a share of commissions for a cut of the equity, you can save 6 percent on the whole transaction as long as you act as both listing and selling agent.

If you end up working with a real estate agent, you will also need to accept the reality of commissions. However, everything is negotiable. You should be able to negotiate a reduced commission for a volume of transactions, and for ensuring that all of your property purchases and sales are run through one agent.

Guidelines for picking the right agent should include:

1. *Find an experienced agent with a track record.* Seek a long-time agent and not just someone who works in the field to earn spending money or fill time. There are several classes of agent, and you need someone who is absolutely professional. You can identify the right agent as someone who has been acknowledged by his or her peers based on sales history; who does thorough research without being asked to; and who knows the market better than anyone else. Also seek a person with professional designations. There are several in addition to the best-known one of Realtor. The National Association of Realtors also licenses people as specialists in various types of real estate.

2. *Do not work with a novice or with an agent selected by default.* Some investors locate agents by walking into a real estate office and talking to the "broker of the day," who quite often is a complete novice. The person taking care of the office may be the latest hire in the firm, the one individual who is not too busy that

day taking care of actual listings. Another poor way to find an agent is by going to open houses. The busiest and most experienced agents often delegate the actual job of showing open houses to novices while they are out getting more listings.

3. *Look for flexibility in the agreement.* Never accept the standard agreement, including a full commission and exclusive listing with the single firm. You need to leave yourself room to negotiate an exceptionally good deal—lower commissions in exchange for a volume of business, incentive compensation for a fast turn-around, and availability of the agent to work with you (including acting as your scout, for example).

4. *Most important of all, find someone who will work with you.* It is not difficult to decide fairly quickly if a person is going to be able to work with you on your terms. You will know, for example, if an agent is relatively inexperienced and knows little or nothing about property flipping. You probably need to work with an agent who specializes in working with investors rather than the more traditional family looking for a long-term primary residence. You need to connect with someone who not only understands the market and the strategy you want to pursue, but who is also a go-getter with excellent research and market knowledge, and who gives you as many ideas and strategies as you have yourself.

buyer's agent

a real estate agent who works for the buyer rather than for the seller, and who is compensated by a fee rather than through commissions.

Some investors like to work with a *buyer's agent*. This is an individual who is hired by the buyer rather than by the seller. Virtually all listing agents are agents for the seller, who pays their commission. A buyer's agent is a consultant in most arrangements, working only for the buyer and, as the argument goes, not subject to the conflicts of interest that most sellers' agents have.

Key Point
The usual argument for hiring a buyer's agent is to get around the conflict of interest arising from how the agent is compensated— usually by the seller. But this is not a big problem if you pick the right person.

The buyer's agent is not necessarily going to provide any better services for you than a seller's agent. It all depends on your ability to find the right person with experience and knowledge of the real estate investment market. A seller's agent is compensated by the seller, but this does not mean that they cannot perform well for you. Using an agent as a scout is an effective way to flip private sales, or to find deep discounts. Some circumstances—estate sales, divorce, foreclosures—can lead to exceptional opportunities, and a seller's agent who brings these deals to you can be effective.

Also remember that if you are going to flip properties in the short term, you will be buyer first and seller second. Therefore, the agent who brings a deal to you actually works for both sides of the transaction. There is every reason to expect that a well-selected seller's agent can perform well for you.

Appraisers, Home Inspectors, and Contractors

Every real estate investor discovers that it is essential to have direct access to a qualified handyman or contractor. For some types of work, a licensed contractor must be used. Specifically, if you will be undertaking major repairs or renovations, you need to work with a company that is licensed and experienced. In practice, though, a handyman (licensed or not) is a far more valuable resource.

By definition, a handyman can fix just about anything and is also affordable. The handyman may not be licensed because the work is done on a less official basis. If you have numerous property interests, a handyman can do small jobs for you with little notice and you will be able to come to agreement concerning the cost without formality. Many real estate investors have found that an amicable (and remunerative) relationship with a handyman makes the entire process work well. One person performs virtually all repair work; that person is easy to work with; and the process is fast and efficient.

Key Point

Flexibility and availability can be more important in a handyman than licensing. But you have to know the risks, and also know when you do need a contractor.

That being said, you do take risks working with anyone who does not have a state license, especially if you do not know the person. You need to balance the practical convenience of working informally with the potential risks if and when work is not performed properly. A lot of work required to meet local code must be approved by your city or county, and that means you have to hire a licensed contractor. While this is more expensive—often unnecessarily so—it is often how the system works. So be sure to make a distinction between private repairs performed without a permit and the more formalized renovation work that has to go through the system.

The same general rule applies to finding qualified inspectors. If your state requires a pest inspection as part of closing, you need to hire someone who is licensed and qualified to inspect property and issue a report. The same goes for specialized inspectors in areas where earthquakes are likely. You may also need to hire a professional home inspector. In such cases, follow these guidelines:

1. *Work with an inspector who issued a written report, without exception.* The service must include a written report, which is an important document. If work is required but not listed on the report, you or a buyer may be able to go back to the inspector and sue to have that company pay to fix the problems.

2. *Be sure the inspector will not also offer to make repairs; only hire an inspector who will not be able to offer additional services.* Anyone who offers to inspect your property *and* perform repairs has an obvious conflict of interest. In additional to making sure the inspector is properly licensed to perform the work, a professional will not offer to make the repairs discovered during the inspection.

3. *Only hire an inspector who will not refer you to anyone to perform repairs.* A conflict of interest also exists if the inspector refers you to someone else. A business associate, friend, or brother-in-law is not necessarily qualified to fix problems with a property, and the

---

Valuable Resource

To find a professional home inspector in your area, check the American Society of Home Inspectors (ASHI) at www.ashi.org. This web site spells out the rules and qualifications of a professional inspector, and allows you to search by ZIP code or metropolitan area.

only way an inspector can remain objective is to stay away from making referrals.

You also will need to work with an appraiser, perhaps on both sides of the transaction. Not all appraisers work in the same way. A local lender, for example, may perform an appraisal by checking local tax records and driving by the house. A more formal approach will involve an inspector's measuring everything and coming into the house to check condition and age of the property.

Depending on who asks for the appraisal and the purpose of that appraisal, the opinion of value can vary significantly. A conservative lender will apply different criteria than a lender who wants to write loans. If you hire an appraiser as part of a divorce, your interest is going to be getting a low appraisal because it will be used as part of a property settlement. So, in spite of what appraisers may claim, the *reason* for the appraisal will affect the outcome.

As a property flipper, you may need to contact an appraiser to work with on your own. This should be someone who meets a few qualifications:

1. *Your appraiser should understand exactly what you need.* You want and need a realistic market value for properties you're thinking of buying. As a potential buyer, you need an honest appraisal to compare to the seller's asked price. This is where you pin down those all-important discounts. This may be especially useful when you need to go to a lender for a short-term loan on property you plan to flip. By showing the lender that market value (as appraised) is much higher than the seller's asked price, it will make it easier to get a loan approved quickly.

2. *A fast response is essential.* If you have to wait several weeks for the results of the appraisal, you will lose opportunities. In some cases, an informal, "ballpark" estimate from a qualified appraiser will be much more valuable than a written opinion with all of the

> **Key Point**
>
> Appraisal is not an exact science, it is an opinion. With this in mind, it is possible to get appraisals at one end or the other of a *reasonable* price range for property.

legal protection. You ultimately need the written appraisal, but find someone willing to help you identify bargains quickly.

3. *Your appraiser needs to understand the importance of flexibility.* When you are the buyer, you need a realistic appraisal estimating market value. When you are a seller, you may seek a more optimistic high-end result. Many sellers provide appraisals to would-be buyers as a "free service." In fact, you may be able to keep prices as high as possible with your own appraisal as long as the estimated value is supported by standard appraisal practices and documented with comparable sales. The latitude an appraiser enjoys is wide, so you need to work with someone who understands how to make the numbers work for you within the law and ethical limits.

Coordinating the Roles of Your Professional Resources

A property flipper needs to get things done quickly. This means a fast turnaround time by real estate agents and an escrow company or attorney; super-fast appraisal results and efficient, fast loan processing; and immediate access to a handyman or contractor.

By bringing together all of the important resources you need to make the deal move quickly, you improve not only your profits but also the range of possible property flipping opportunities. If it takes too long to put a deal together, you may lose a large percentage of them. If you can make it all happen quickly, you are in a better competitive position and you will be able to also cut costs involved in transactions.

> **Key Point**
>
> You speed up the whole flipping experience by lining up flexible professional resources. The right people can save thousands of dollars and make the process move quickly.

Let's say you work with an escrow department, real estate agent, and lender who can move quickly. And let's say you can find a buyer before your initial escrow even closes. With the cooperation of everyone involved, you could buy *and* sell the property with a single escrow, title search, title insurance policy, and document and filing fees. Your lender might be willing to finance your purchase for a minimum fee only to end up not needing to go any farther because the new buyer gets his or her own financing. This type of arrangement makes things go quickly and saves thousands of dollars on real estate transactions.

Getting to the point where your participation as scout, dealer, or retailer is working at maximum efficiency as well as your ability to line up your resources takes time and experience. The more you develop this personal network of valuable resources, the better poised you are to make the most of the property flipping experience.

The next chapter, on real estate options, shows you a way to acquire the rights to property without taking title and thus expand your potential investment profits substantially.

Chapter 4

The Ultimate Leverage Magic

Using Lease Options to Flip Property

Most people understand how the traditional real estate contract works. It requires two sides, a buyer and a seller, to come to a mutual agreement on price and other terms. This *meeting of the minds* is one of the requirements for a contract to become valid.

The real estate contract is typical of a *bilateral contract* or one in which both sides are part of the agreement. This type of contract requires that the buyer agrees to buy property and the seller agrees to sell. There is also another type of contract in which only one side is bound to perform but the other is not. This is called a *unilateral contract*.

A real estate contract is usually bilateral. Another type that is valuable to property flippers is a unilateral contract: the *purchase option*. Under this agreement, you pay a property owner for the right to buy, but you are not required to exercise that right. The option has no tangible value, and exists only as a right. It expires at a specified date in the

meeting of the minds
the agreement between two sides in a contract, which can include the price, deadlines, and other terms needed to create a valid and binding contract.

bilateral contract
a type of contract in which both sides are required to perform; for example, a buyer agrees to pay for property, and a seller agrees to relinquish title.

> ### Key Point
>
> An option is not a tangible asset, just a contractual right. But properly used, an option can provide you with maximum leverage.

unilateral contract

a type of contract binding one side to perform but not the other. For example, if a seller is required to sell under the terms of a contract but the buyer is not required to buy, the agreement is unilateral.

purchase option

an option granting the option owner the right, but not the obligation, to purchase property at a specified price and by a specified time. If the option is not exercised by the date indicated, it expires and becomes worthless.

future and, if you do not exercise the option by that date, the option expires.

Property flipping can be accomplished with the use of options and can serve as an effective tool for holding the right to property without having to take title. If the real estate market is flat or declines in the future, you simply allow the option to expire. If values rise, you can exercise the option and make an immediate profit. For example, if you purchase an option from a property owner to buy the property within three years at a price of $150,000, you must exercise before the period expires. If at the end of the period the property is worth only $120,000, you would not exercise; your option would simply expire. However, if values have risen and the property is worth $225,000, you would exercise the option and buy the property at the agreed-upon price of $150,000.

The Traditional Sequence: Buy, Hold, Sell

For many people, options sound too good to be true. Why would a property owner sell you the right to buy property at a fixed price, given the possibility that values could rise? There may be several reasons, including:

1. *Immediate cash.* The option is paid for by its owner. So if you approach someone who owns a piece of land, and you offer to buy an option, the deal will include a payment of cash, either up front or in a series of installments. For the property owner, the option is "free" money in the sense that nothing has to be given

in exchange at the moment; the prospect of transferring title at a future date may seem remote in comparison to getting cash in hand immediately.

2. *The combination of the option with a lease.* The typical use of options is in combination with a lease agreement. The *lease option* is a contract with two parts. The lease is an agreement to pay rent to the owner, and the option is a grant of rights. This is often used in situations where someone agrees to buy property but does not have a down payment. The option portion of the monthly payment goes toward the down payment over a period of time, and at the end of the lease, the sale is completed. For the property owner, a lease option may be a desirable way to transfer property. While market rent may be $800, a lease option may produce a much higher monthly payment.

> **lease option**
> a contract between a property owner and a tenant (or prospective buyer). The lease is a rental contract and the option grants the right to the leaseholder to purchase property at a fixed price before the expiration date.

3. *A belief that values will not rise within the option term.* Some property owners will gladly sell an option to increase rental income in the immediate future, in the belief that property values will not rise. The risk to the property owner is that future equity may be lost; the risk to the option buyer is that future values may not rise.

4. *A method of selling property in a slow market.* The option (or a lease option) may be viewed by current owners as an advantageous way to sell property in a slow real estate market. The inability to find a market-rate buyer may be offset by offering a lease option. Someone who is willing to speculate on future real estate values (or who sees an opportunity to flip the property) will be attracted to the lease option.

The traditional way to manage real estate or any other investment follows a very predictable course of events. First you buy; then you hold the property for a period of time; finally, you sell. In fact, this sequence applies to virtually all purchases made by investors and consumers. But it is not the only way.

> ### Key Point
>
> When you take the traditional approach (buy, hold, sell) you expose yourself to a range of investment risks. Most of these risks are eliminated with the strategic use of options.

One problem with this traditional method (buy, hold, sell) is that it exposes you to unpredictable market forces. You might buy today only to have property values go flat or even drop in the future. In that case, the entire premise for investing fails. You lose money or you need to hold the property longer than you wanted to, just to wait out the real estate supply-and-demand cycle. This problem is experienced by all investors. If you buy stock and the share price falls, you have three choices: wait out the market, sell at a loss, or buy more shares. Stock investors would always prefer that prices rise right after they buy shares.

So the market risk—the risk that prices will not rise after you buy— is a serious concern in real estate as well as in all investments. If you enter an investment program with the assumption that prices are going to rise, that assumption should be based on some facts. If you have studied the market and you believe that there are sound justifications to believe prices will rise, then the chance is worth taking. But if you have performed no real market research, then investing is really a form of gambling. This makes the point that investors always face risk in one form or another; but the risk can be reduced by performing research and by analyzing the market and the product beforehand.

The problem all goes back to that traditional sequence of steps— buy, hold, and sell—that most people believe is the only method for acquiring the investment. The option poses an alternative to this traditional approach *and* to the risks it involves.

The Option Sequence: Hold, Exercise, Profit

The interesting aspect of options for property flippers is that they provide maximum leverage with minimum risk. In the traditional buy-hold-sell transaction, you need to put capital at risk by taking an equity position in property. Thus, all real estate investors using the traditional approach experience considerable risk. If property values do not rise, you face the prospect of loss or having to convert a speculative flip into a long-term rental. The trade-off—historical price appreciation, tax advantages, and insurability of the investment among the significant advantages—often makes the risk worthwhile. But using options allows you to avoid that risk altogether.

Options are not used widely because many people simply do not understand how they work. Sellers may not be willing to commit themselves to options either because it means they do not get to sell the property until some date in the future and, even then, because the option agreement is a unilateral contract, it might not happen at all. The fact is that options are rarely more beneficial for sellers than for buyers.

Options provide you maximum leverage in several respects:

1. *The option fixes the purchase price.* The primary feature of the option is that it sets the price by contract, but does not require you to close the deal. The property owner gives up the right to future appreciation (if that occurs) in exchange for the *option premium* you pay. That premium buys you the right to exercise if you wish. The contract also contains an expiration date. So if you do exercise, that has to occur before the option expires.

2. *Little or no money is required up front.* The option can be structured so that you end up without any cash at risk. For example, if you can sublease the property to cover your obligation to the owner, you end up without any payout of cash. You assume the usual landlord risks. If your tenant does not pay or if you experience vacancies, your obligation continues. Yet as long as your tenant pays you, the option cost will be zero or less. At the same time, because you have absolutely no equity position in the property, you are not directly responsible for taxes, insurance, mortgage payments, or repairs. (To the extent

> **option premium**
> the amount paid by the person acquiring an option to the property owner. The premium is paid in exchange for fixing the price of property in the event the option is exercised.

Key Point

Getting a contract agreeing to a *future* price of real estate is a powerful advantage—and worth the cost of an option.

> ### Key Point
>
> The option is one of the few ways to acquire property with no money down, meaning your investment risk is reduced to nearly zero.

that you are acting as landlord to a tenant, you have the obligation to cover utilities and routine maintenance; but the owner has the same obligation to you.)

3. *Using options gives you the potential to maintain control over many properties without needing to qualify for financing.* Most real estate investors have to limit their risk to only a few properties, usually three or four at the most. This is so not only because down payment money is limited (and higher down payment is often required for investors than for homeowners). Lenders also have limits in the number of positions on which they can loan mortgage money. However, as an option holder, you have no equity position and no need for loans. At the same time, you have set the price on property for minimal cash outlay. In theory, there is no limit on the number of option properties you can control except for the difficulty in locating property owners willing to grant options.

Risks are kept minimal with options because you are not required to take up an equity position in property. You are not required to exercise the option. Depending on how the option is priced, you may have no net cash outlay whatsoever, yet still fix the price of the property, if and when you decide to exercise the option.

How Options Work: The Details

Given the features of the real estate option—granting you the right to buy property at a fixed price and before a specific date—it makes sense to get the lowest possible contractual price for the longest possible period. It is also

> ### Key Point
>
> Lenders say no to investors who want to pick up large numbers of properties. With options, you do not even need to borrow money. You avoid the limitations of financing altogether.

likely that the longer the term you want to reserve that price, the more you will be required to pay for the option.

The specific pricing of options is elusive and there is no universal formula. Some real estate insiders will try to claim that options should be based on a percentage of the fixed price stated in the contract, but that is not realistic for several reasons:

1. *The option price might be higher than current market value.* If the option's specified sale price of property were always the current market value, it might be easy to set the value of the option premium itself. But the stated purchase price is usually somewhere above current market value, and that varies as well. If there were any kind of cause and effect in real estate options, two factors would determine premium value:

   • The time between the option origination date and expiration would be the first factor.
   • The second factor would be the dollar difference between current market value of the property and the contractual agreed-upon price if and when the option is exercised.

   While options on stocks are traded in an orderly manner on the stock exchanges where these factors do determine premium value, there is no such market uniformity for real estate options.

2. *Not all markets are the same, so a fixed percentage is not realistic.* You cannot set a single percentage for option premium based on some universal standard because all markets are different. For example, in a very slow, depressed market, owners may be quite willing to grant options for low prices. In a very hot market, owners would tend to want more premium and a higher option price.

3. *Actual option value is negotiated between current owner and you.* How desperate are you to get the option? And how willing (or desperate) is the property owner? The motivation of each side ultimately determines the value of the option.

Key Point

A negotiated value of the option will be based on the range between the exercise price of the option and the real or perceived current market value of the property.

Using options is one way to get started in property flipping without a lot of cash. Start by checking want ads and seeing what current owners are offering. If you cannot find option opportunities listed, put your own ad in the paper; talk to real estate agents; or network among landlords, business associations, and builders' exchanges. Talk to local developers and contractors, and let the word get out that you are interested in purchasing options on local properties.

Typically, the lease option is valued in terms of a monthly payment. You may find a rental house that the owner is willing to lease to you with an option for a higher monthly payment than current rental value. If rental rates are $1,000, you may be able to get a two-year option for $1,300 per month. In writing up a lease agreement, all of the terms of the agreement are spelled out, including how much of the monthly payment is for rent and how much goes toward the option.

Because the option is an encumbrance on the property (just like a mortgage or other lien in the sense that it places an obligation on the owner), it has to be recorded. This is usually done at a County Recorder's office and a specific form may be required. For any lease option or straight option agreement, you need the help of an attorney or a knowledgeable escrow officer to ensure that the proper paperwork is completed and recorded according to the law.

Figure 4.1 summarizes the choices you have to make if you purchase an option on property. In addition to the possibilities of exercising or not exercising, the option can also be extended or renegotiated on terms that both sides find agreeable.

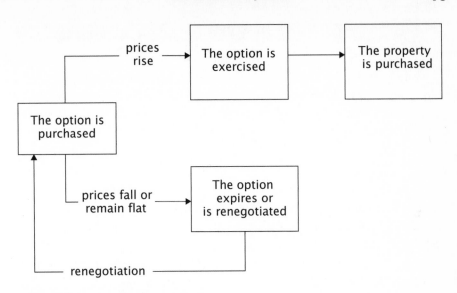

FIGURE 4.1   Purchasing an Option

The Risks of Options

Everyone in a real estate transactions—current owners as well as property flippers—must be aware of the risks involved in the use of options. If they are not executed correctly or the right forms are not used, the option might not be enforceable. If the option is not recorded, it might also fail the test of a true instrument. Legal advice is definitely required in order to execute the option.

Some real estate dealers—or more precisely, wheeler-dealers—use option-like methods to pick up real estate at deep discounts. This trick works when the market is soft and owners want to sell, so they accept an offer. But rather than offering a formal offer, the dealer proposes to pay all cash, which, of course, is very appealing to the owner.

Key Point
If you are going to get involved in options, you need legal advice to make sure everything is done correctly. Also, be aware that there are some unscrupulous people out there trying to take advantage of owners and investors, and they may also use options.

> ## Key Point
>
> From a seller's point of view, the promise of an "all cash deal" is very exciting. In reality, upon sale you get all cash regardless of whether the buyer has the money or gets a loan. Virtually every real estate agent knows a cash buyer or claims to; and many unethical players try to tempt owners with promises of an all-cash deal.

The flaw in the all-cash deal is that you as a seller get all cash even if the buyer has to find a lender. The argument is often a distraction intended to persuade a seller of the seriousness of the offer. In practice, the deal does not work out well for the seller.

The all-cash argument is meant to elicit a nice discount from market value. So a seller agrees to the terms. But the buyer next demands an exceptionally long escrow. Rather than the usual 30- to 60-day period, the buyer demands, for example, a six-month escrow. Accompanied by a relatively small *earnest money* deposit, the would-be buyer explains that it will take time to complete the sale of another property or settle a relative's estate. If, during the six-month period, the value of the property rises, the buyer can buy the property at a discount from the original price, but at a very deep discount off market value. Meanwhile, he may find a buyer to come into the picture by the end of six months and buy the property at full market value.

In practice, the unethical wheeler-dealer in this situation has managed to get a six-month option on the property for the cost of an earnest money deposit (or for no cost if the deal goes through). Not only that; the option price was discounted in exchange for the promise of an all-cash deal.

earnest money

a deposit made by a purchaser as part of a real estate contract in order to establish his or her seriousness about the deal. If the buyer backs out of the contract, the earnest money deposit is forfeited.

> ## Key Point
>
> Be aware of those asking for unusually long escrow periods, and do not be swayed by the promise of an all-cash deal.

While arrangements like this occur, it is easy to avoid them. Any special deals or arrangements that involve excessively long escrow periods or low earnest money deposits should be avoided.

Any situation in which you purchase the right to property will contain risks for both sides. The property owner, faced with the offer of an option, is concerned with performance as well as potential loss of future value. You can make the offer more attractive—thus reducing apprehension—with certain provisions such as an offer to pay rent several months in advance. If you are asking for an option close to current market value of the property, you may need to shorten the time frame. Or if you need more time to let the market value appreciate, you may have to increase the exercise price. The whole negotiation is a matter of give and take for both sides. But you need to develop insight into what the owner wants right now. If the owner does not want to deal with tenants who pay rent late every month, prepayment of rent is one practical solution. If the owner believes the market is flat and prices will never rise, a longer-term lease may be a suitable resolution for the owner. If the property is run-down and in need of work, making your offer without contingencies for repairs may also be very appealing.

The typical lease option used by someone who wants to buy their first home (but does not have a down payment) would be entered for different reasons than those reasons of a property flipper. In general, a straightforward option used by someone who wants to purchase a property follows a predictable course. If property values rise above the exercise price, you would indeed exercise the option and buy the property. If values remain at or below the price, you would not exercise. This brings up the most promising application for options: property flipping with little or no money down. This can be done honestly and using options without needing to trick a seller into a long escrow period.

Options with No Money Down

Property flipping is usually restricted by the considerations of available capital and financing. Most people cannot afford to flip numerous properties at the same time through the traditional route—buy, hold, sell—because lenders will simply not extend credit indefinitely. Options overcome this problem.

It is possible to control and earn profits from several properties without needing to make a down payment or take ownership. Options

Key Point
You can use options to maximize your profits without ever taking an equity position. This is especially advantageous when real estate markets are robust and prices are rising.

allow you to position yourself to participate in a rising market with several properties without the risks. Consider what is possible if you identify discounted property opportunities and work within a specific time frame.

For example, you locate a property that you believe has potential for future growth. Typical prices for similar homes are $125,000 but this property has been listed for several months and did not receive any offers. The listing recently expired. The owner is discouraged because the property did not sell. Your perception is that the market is slow at the moment but will be robust within two to three years. So you offer to purchase an option and to lease the property from the owner.

Let us say that market rents are approximately $750 per month. You offer to pay the owner $900 per month in a three-year lease, with $750 in rent and $150 per month in an option. You have the right to buy the property at any time within three years for $100,000. The owner accepts your terms. You sign the three-year lease and immediately rent the property out to a family for $1,000 per month *under a lease option*. The terms you provide include rent of $750 per month and an option of $250 per month, which gives the renters the opportunity to purchase the property at $135,000 within three years.

In this situation, you have paid out no money. In fact, you will be receiving $100 per month more than you are paying. You have no equity position, thus no responsibility for property taxes, insurance, or utilities. (The owner may pay some of the utilities directly, but you do not have to.) If market values rise above your option's level of $100,000 and you exercise your option, you acquire the property at a profit. If property values do not rise above $135,000, your tenant will not exercise the second option; and if prices rise above $135,000 both options are exercised.

If no options are exercised, you end up the 36-month period with no loss and with a net gain of $100 per month. The lease expires and everything returns to the way it was before (unless the options are renegotiated). If the value of the property rises above $100,000, you will make a profit whether or not your tenant also exercises. But that will not happen unless values rise above $135,000. So you cannot lose in this transaction.

Two options are involved, so the possibilities are more complex than they would be if you simply exercised a single option and then tried to market the property. The advantage here is that you never need to take an equity position. You coordinate the two transactions in a single escrow and, if all goes well, you walk away with a check for $35,000 less some small fees ($35,000 is the difference between the exercise prices of the two options). Ideally, you should not have to pay many of the fees, since you have both a buyer and a seller, who should share in those fees. As a conduit between the two sides, you act as dealer and never assume any equity positions or responsibility for closing or escrow costs.

If you employ only a single option in this transaction, several differences have to be noted. First, you will be paying out $150 per month, the difference between rental value and your lease option. This assumes you rent the property to someone for market rate of $750 per month. But there is a more important difference here. When your tenant also has a second lease option, he or she is building a *contingent equity interest* in the property. They are less likely to walk away without exercising their option, especially when property values are rising. So while a tenant might move without a second thought, a tenant in a lease option has a far different point of view. They are also more likely to care for the property as if it were their own, because it is likely to become their property within three years.

> **contingent equity interest**
> the interest a tenant has in a property when part of a lease option, which is strengthened as property values rise; or the interest that any owner of an option has in property based on growing market value and potential exercise.

Another difference is cash flow. In the dual-option arrangement, you create a situation where you gain each month, but if you simply purchased on option and rented out the property, you would need to absorb the difference in cash.

Key Point

Using the double option strategy, you pass cash flow risk and market risk through from the current owner to the tenant. Acting as dealer, you avoid most of the risks entirely.

The level of risk is also quite different. The dual option literally passes your investment risk on to your tenant. Throughout this process, you do not need to take on any of the risks of ownership, including on-going expenses and debt repayments, or responsibility for repairs. Because you sublease the property to someone else, you act as a dealer. And because you do not need to obtain financing, there is no limitation on how many of these deals you could put together.

What if property values fall? In this worst-case scenario, you would lose money if you were working with a single option only. The premium you pay to the owner would be gone. But because you also sell an option to someone else, you eliminate the risk altogether. If property values remain below the exercise price of your option, the whole deal simply evaporates. The lease term ends and you walk away. If the property value ends up somewhere between the two option prices, you still have the right to exercise your option, but your tenant will not do the same. You may either cancel the lease option or renegotiate its terms.

It is quite difficult to arrange a dual-option transaction such as the one described above. It is possible, but difficult. A more typical transaction involves your actually taking possession of the property as direct tenant under a lease with an option—or as the leaseholder who subsequently subleases the property. In the first instance, you pay monthly rent and option premium to the landlord/owner. In the second, you act as conduit and make your monthly payments from the rent you charge to your tenant.

At some point before expiration of your option, you advertise the property and sell it. As long as your option exercise price is below current market value, you will be able to realize a profit in this transaction. The option is exercised during the course of escrow. There are four parties involved in this transaction:

1. The current owner of property who has sold you the option.

2. You as tenant under a lease, as owner of the option, and as landlord in the sublease.

3. The tenant who either rents month to month or under a lease that you have signed with that tenant.

4. The buyer (who may or may not be your tenant) who acquires title to the property during escrow. Title passes from the current owner to the buyer, and you release your option as part of the

transaction, which entitles you to a profit (the difference between the net sales price and your option exercise price). So if the option is for $100,000 and the contractual sales price is $145,000, you are entitled to the difference less any fees coming out of the sale. The current owner is entitled to $100,000 minus any fees and liens on the property.

As this example demonstrates, the lease option is a powerful tool for property flipping. However, it may be difficult to find current owners willing to take part in such a deal. These are complex transactions and some people are frightened off by the option approach. If you do locate willing owners, there is no limit to how many options you can buy, especially through a two-part lease option arrangement.

The next chapter discusses another strategy: the conversion. Even when you begin with the idea of a fast in-and-out transaction, you might discover it is advantageous to hold on to some properties and wait out the real estate market.

Conversion Strategies
From Flip to Hold

When you enter into a property flipping strategy—or any investment plan—you work from a set of assumptions. You expect things to go in a specific manner. If you are right, the outcome will also meet your expectations. As every investor knows, however, these plans do not always work out. Property flipping may need to be structured to allow for the possibility of converting from flipping to a hold pattern for a brief period of time.

The contingency planning should include consideration of the following major issues:

1. *Long-term versus short-term financing.* You may make arrangements with a lender for extremely short-term financing as part of a property flipping strategy. Some lenders will work with real estate speculators to provide such loan guarantees, knowing that equity positions, if any, will last only a few days or weeks. Many property flipping plans call for selling property before the purchase even closes, so financing is a secondary concern—most of the time. However, if your strategy does not work out as planned, you will need to be able to put more permanent mortgage financing plans into place. As part of your contingency planning, you

Key Point
Every investor starts out with a set of assumptions, which makes sense. But remember, assumptions are not always correct.

will need to be in contact with a lender who is willing to approve a loan for investment property if and when you need it.

2. *Cash flow and a study of current market rental levels.* You need to know the market rent level for the kinds of properties you intend to flip. If current market rates are too low to cover cash flow—in the event you hold on to property longer than originally planned—you could face a bad situation. If your cash outflow is higher than income, how will you recover that loss? How long will it take? Can you afford it? If so, what dollar amount could you absorb if you convert from flipping to rental?

3. *Policies about how to find, screen, and work with tenants.* If you convert a flip property to a rental, how will you find tenants? How will you screen them? Will you deal with tenants directly or hire a management company?

    You will need access to forms for application, property condition, and rental contract, and you will also need to decide how you plan to check references, how much deposit to collect, and whether to enter a lease agreement or month-to-month rental contract. For anyone not familiar with landlord and tenant issues, a management company can provide invaluable help and guidance.

4. *Overall portfolio management, asset allocation, and cash flow questions.* In looking at your overall portfolio, you may have a concept about how property flipping fits in the larger plan. But how does the more illiquid long-term real estate investment fit?

How much down payment will you need to tie up in real estate and for how long? What is the impact of holding real estate on your overall allocation strategy? If you do not plan ahead to anticipate how real estate may impact your overall portfolio, an unanticipated conversion could become a problem in terms not only of cash flow but also for your individual financial plan. These are question you will want to address before you pick properties in order to ensure that, in the worst-case outcome, you have anticipated the most obvious changes a conversion will involve.

Market Cycles and Changes

A good starting point is an in-depth study of the real estate market in your region. This gives you insight into the trend in pricing and the viability of a property flipping strategy (as well as how well a conversion strategy is likely to play out in the same market).

The purpose of analyzing the local market in considerable detail is twofold. First, you need to become the expert on your real estate market in order to place yourself in the best position to recognize property flipping opportunities. Second, you also need to be as well prepared as possible for contingency planning—meaning you need to also understand rental demand levels, vacancy rates, strength or weakness of the overall market, financing rates and availability of mortgage money, and construction projects under way and planned. All of these factors affect the market directly.

Markets change, of course. So even if you did all of your homework last year, these analyses are ongoing. Just as stock market investors need to study their list of stocks from week to week, real estate investors also need to keep track of market trends. In fact, there are actually three different real estate markets you need to watch:

- The well-known price market
- The rental market
- The financing market

These three markets operate independently to a degree. You may find that prices for real estate are rising, but rental demand is very soft—or vice versa. In some communities, a strong rental demand exists that operates separately from the supply and demand for owner-occupied housing such as relatively small cities with large university populations. Financing—consisting of money available to lend and the interest rates in effect—varies as well. At times, lenders impose very high costs for

---

Key Point

Analysis of your local market provides two benefits. First, as a local expert, you are well positioned to recognize value and opportunities. Second, the same knowledge helps you with the all-important contingency planning every investor needs.

borrowing money (consisting not only of a high rate but also in points and other fees); but when money is plentiful and lenders actively seek business, they tend to make more attractive offers (e.g., low-cost closing, free appraisal, or fast turnaround on approval).

The major market factors operate together as well, and in many communities you find that demand for housing tracks rental and financing markets closely. The actual conditions in your market depend on many variables, including employment trends, population growth or decline, and projects under construction. The economic condition of the overall real estate market today can be judged by observing several statistical and economic trends, including:

1. *The market sales statistics.* One way to spot trends as they develop is to seek out subtle changes in the three statistics about today's housing demands. The spread (the difference between listed price and sales price), inventory (months of housing presently on the market based on demand levels), and time on market (the number of weeks or months the average property takes to sell) are useful as static outcomes. They are even more revealing when studied over time. As these trends grow and change, you can recognize the emerging supply and demand trend. These statistics can be found through local multiple listing service (MLS) offices or subscriber real estate professionals and lenders.

2. *Construction trends.* If you have seen a gradual increase in property values in an area where little or no new construction has taken place, that is usually seen as a positive trend. A limited supply matched against strong demand invariably leads to higher prices.

   But what happens if a major new subdivision is being planned? If your community has experienced 400 new sales per year and a developer is planning to complete a 500-unit subdivision by next spring, what does that mean? Real estate prices will be flat for at least one year and possibly more. It is even possible that prices may fall if the developer is offering units below typical market rates

---

Key Point

Sales statistics are the most immediate and dependable sources for identifying the strength or weakness of your local market today.

Key Point

Investors may focus on historical price trends exclusively—and forget to keep an eye on construction. Consider the impact on housing prices of a major new subdivision that may be completed next year.

---

in effect. Current and planned construction projects can also affect today's trend. If demand outpaces supply and no major projects are planned, the upward trend is likely to continue. However, other factors, such as decreasing employment, also affect value.

3. *Rental trends.* The rental market is not always going to track the overall supply-and-demand market. It is affected by prices, however. For example, in areas where prices of housing have risen substantially, it may be impossible to make cash flow work by purchasing homes. In Manhattan, San Francisco, or Los Angeles, for example, where housing easily exceeds $600,000, mortgage payments will likely be so much higher than market rents that the entire rental market is restricted. Only those who have no mortgages (mostly people who are long-term owners) can afford to rent out property at market rates. And even though market rates may be exceptionally high, they are not always high enough to cover cash flow. In those high-priced areas, mortgage payments may be as high as $5,000 per month, and market rental rates for housing only $3,000 to $4,000.

Trends can also operate in reverse. When rental demand is high, rents rise in response. So in a community with little demand for housing, a high rental demand may coexist with a relatively flat pricing market. A community characterized by a combination of retirement-aged couples and singles and college students would meet this model. It would be characterized by low demand for owner-occupied housing (thus, little if any growth in property values) and a very high demand for rental housing.

Key Point

The rental market is entirely separate from the supply-and-demand market for housing. These two markets may change in tandem or move in completely opposite directions.

---

4. *The financing market.* Many investors are aware of the markets for housing and rentals, but not of the financing market. As with all commodities, the supply of money available to place into mortgages varies with fiscal policies at the federal level, and with institutional policies among conventional lenders (not to mention supply and demand in the mortgage secondary market, where mortgage pools are created and shares sold to investors through GNMA and FNMA and similar quasi-governmental organizations).

As mortgage money becomes more available, lender policies also become more liberal. This is a positive attribute for investors for two reasons. First and most obvious, more availability of money means you are able to make better and more economical decisions for yourself. Second, it becomes easier for investors to get loans even when competing with homeowners. Generally, homeowners who will occupy properties they finance can get 90 percent (and even 100 percent) financing, and when money is available it is easy for buyers to qualify. Investors are likely to be asked to make larger down payments of 20 to 30 percent and also to pay higher interest rates. The analysis of your loan application is also done more critically for investment property, notably in the study of potential cash flow. So investors are most affected by a changing market for financing of investments. It is one version of supply and demand that is easily overlooked.

In the stock market, the usual advice people hear is "buy low and sell high." In real estate, a modification of this advice is worth thinking about: "Buy when the market is cold, and sell when the market is hot." Just as it makes sense to buy depressed stocks and wait for them to double before selling, real estate also goes through predictable cycles. These are affected by predictable events and the cause and effect of real estate is the same as with any other market. Growing or shrinking employment and demographic changes, interest rates, construction trends, and changing preferences in housing design are among the dozens of possible

---

Key Point

Recent history has demonstrated that real estate prices can be influenced significantly by interest rates and availability of mortgage money. This is the most important contributing factor to any housing bubble.

factors affecting the value of real estate. Recognition of the real estate cycle and how the trends are moving is a key to:

1. Knowing where the market is today.
2. Seeing where it is moving.
3. Positioning yourself to minimize property flipping risks; all depends on your astute observations of the market.

Short-term cycles are chaotic, and it may be difficult to judge the economic cycle of real estate in a week-to-week pattern. This is why you need to view a broader regional trend that includes many different factors, even beyond real estate itself. So while construction trends and recent price movement are important, so are local demographic and economic factors. When you view the whole picture, you are far more likely to be able to reduce risks and make informed decisions.

The Buy-and-Hold Strategy

When you start a *buy-and-hold strategy*—whether intentionally or because the initial property flipping strategy needs to be changed—you face a new set of investment criteria. Unlike the flipping concept, which is usually short term in nature, the buy-and-hold strategy requires several different strategic applications. These include:

1. *Comparative "pro-and-con" study between flipping and buy-and-hold.* Investors tend to make mental pro-and-con lists, which is one way of identifying risk levels and determining whether the profit potential is worthwhile. The key for property flippers who may become buy-and-hold investors is to recognize that the risk and profit attributes for these two approaches are vastly different; so the comparative analysis needs to be performed for both flipping and buy-and-hold, and then the two lists need to be compared and studied with the whole range of possible outcomes in mind.

buy-and-hold strategy
a strategy for acquiring real estate in which property is acquired and rented out, to be sold when prices are higher. In the ideal buy-and-hold situation, rent is adequate to make mortgage payments and to pay for property taxes, insurance, utilities, and maintenance costs.

Key Point

Not only are flipping and buy-and-hold different investment strategies, they also require different analyses and contingency planning.

---

2. *Long-term planning for investment cash flow.* If you can achieve short-term property flipping without needing to take an equity position (or owning properties only for a very short time), then your orientation toward cash flow is limited and rightly so. If you end up in a buy-and-hold strategy, you will need to plan your cash flow far more extensively.

3. *A different range of contingency plans.* The property flipper is mainly concerned with finding buyers willing to pay for their properties— ideally at a level that will produce a profit on a short-term basis. The contingency with flipping is that the market trend may slow or stop, or the conclusion of the deal may not be profitable or happen in the desired time frame. With buy-and-hold strategies, an entirely different list of contingencies has to be developed, studied, and planned for. These include concern for the trend in market prices (but over an expanded time frame), basic cash flow concerns, trends in vacancies and changes in market rental rates, financing, tying up capital you originally may have planned to use elsewhere, and the whole range of tenant-related issues.

4. *Asset allocation adjustments in some instances.* If you approach investing by allocating assets, a change in strategy can throw your plan into disarray. You may have your portfolio divided among stocks at 40 percent, savings and liquid money market funds at 15 percent, and real estate (consisting of your home) at 40 percent. The remaining 5 percent is used for your property flipping ventures. However, if you end up having to tie up capital in a converted buy-and-hold strategy, you find yourself needing to make a down payment and live with a long-term mortgage. Even if the ongoing cash requirements are covered by rent, this situation still upsets your carefully planned asset allocation program. You might find yourself 60 or 65 percent in real estate in spite of your desire to keep real estate at or below 40 percent.

Key Point

A change in strategies for real estate investing is likely to impact an asset allocation plan. This should be considered as part of your contingency planning, if only to be aware of the possibility of that impact.

In this situation, you face a decision. Either you have to live with the change in allocation in a belief that supply and demand will redeem the strategy, or you may need to figure out how to sell the property to realign your portfolio. This decision should be made depending on how seriously you view the change to your allocation plan.

5. *Overall evaluation of real estate in your portfolio as either speculative play or long-term conservative hold.* The property flipper is more often than not a speculator, interested in making a short-term profit in real estate. Acting as a dealer, a real estate property flipper may never take up an equity position, so that risk exposure is minimal at any given time. In comparison, the long-term investor is more conservative and may view real estate as an appreciating asset. Growth will vary between 3 percent and 12 percent per year, and the long-term investor is willing to manage tenants in the interim to benefit from holding property for many years.

Clearly, the vast differences in profile between property flipping and buy-and-hold require careful evaluation of your entire investment portfolio. You need to ensure that any strategies you use (whether intentionally or as a contingency plan) are appropriate in your portfolio. Some investors like to allocate not only among products but also by risk features. You might consider dividing your portfolio between conservative growth stocks and your own home, and more speculative market plays such as the stock options market and property flipping. The division of a portfolio by risk attributes is just as appropriate as allocation by product type and works for many investors who cannot settle completely for one strategic view or the other.

Converting the Flipping Strategy: Property Selection Criteria

When you consider property flipping as an investment strategy—without any contingent planning—the concept is easy to understand. You buy at a discount and sell at retail as quickly as possible and walk away with a profit. In practice, however, you do need to allow for the greatest contingency of all—that you will not be able to sell the property as quickly as you want or for the markup you expect.

Because of this, you need to pick properties with two sets of criteria. First, the price has to be discounted enough to justify the property flip. (This requirement is also based on the assumption that the market is strong enough to support the flipping strategy itself.) Second, if and when you end up converting to a long-term hold, you need to ensure that the rental market is strong enough to provide the cash flow you will need.

A brief look at the first requirement should include the possibility that today's real estate market may not be growing by leaps and bounds. This does *not* preclude property flipping as a strategy. You can profit from trading in *distressed properties* as well as seeking discounts in a rapidly growing market. A distressed property is one in need of repairs or in which the current owner is seriously behind in payments or even in default.

distressed properties

any properties needing repairs, often of a serious nature; or those properties whose owners are experiencing financial problems or urgency to sell.

The distress itself is most often associated with property condition. A house that has been trashed or allowed to fall into disrepair fits this description. But distress can also refer to the owner's financial problems. For example, an individual who cannot afford to keep up with payments or is already in default is distressed on a personal level and may be quite willing to sell at a discount just to get out of the obligation. Distress may also be the result of personal bankruptcy, divorce, or the death of a family member. All of these personal causes of

---

Key Point

Most contingency plans are based on what you need to do when things go wrong. This applies in all markets—stocks, mutual funds, and even real estate.

> ### Key Point
>
> If you look for distressed property (and distressed property owners), you may provide a solution for everyone concerned—and still make a profit on the transaction.

distress represent flipping opportunities. This does not mean the property flipper is taking advantage of someone else. If a discounted price is agreeable to everyone, then a property flipper can enter the picture between lender and owner and offer the perfect solution to everyone's problems.

The second set of criteria in picking properties to flip has to include the anticipation that the property may end up as a rental property—even when you prefer to move in and out of position and make a fast profit. Thus, the contingency has to include an evaluation of the current rental market. If it is possible that you will end up holding the property, you might need to wait out the market. If this does happen, you will need to ask the following series of financial and risk-based questions:

1. *How will the purchase be financed?* Perhaps the most urgent, immediate question is how you would finance a purchase. With the concept of flipping a property short term, you may be able to find a lender who understands its role as one of guaranteeing financing, without actually writing a permanent mortgage loan. You may create and access a home equity line of credit to use for earnest money deposits and down payments, based on the fast turnaround of property ownership. But what happens if you end up keeping the property?

2. *What are current market rents for properties like this?* A study of your local rental market will reveal typical rental rates for properties like the one you plan to flip. Be aware of subtle differences within the market. In a city with a large college population, properties located close to the university will be desirable as student rentals. Duplex or triplex units may provide far better cash flow than single-family houses. And housing generally commands much higher rents than apartments. Finally, slight variations between neighborhoods and available amenities make significant differences in market rents (access to transportation, schools, shopping, and entertainment, or levels of noise all come into the equation).

Key Point

A conversion studied as part of your contingency plan is not entirely negative. When you consider potential growth in market value, reduced taxes on gains, and significant tax advantages to holding property, the conversion can be a very profitable alternative.

---

3. *What is the typical vacancy rate and trend?* You also need to evaluate the current vacancy rates and the ongoing trend. Are vacancies growing or shrinking? This is perhaps the most important statistic locally for the rental market, and it is available through local rental services and property management firms, as well as economic development departments of the local government. If vacancy rates are below 5 percent and remaining steady or dropping, that indicates a very strong market. If the rates are higher and increasing (due to overconstruction of rental units, for example), then you may experience cash flow problems due to extended vacancies or find that you are not able to get market rents adequate to cover your cash flow requirements.

passive loss
the loss from investments in which the investor is not actively involved such as limited partnerships or real estate. Losses generally cannot be deducted but have to be carried forward and applied against future passive gains. One exception involves directly owned real estate; investors may deduct up to $25,000 per year in losses.

4. *How much cash will be tied up in the property?* If you convert from short-term flip to long-term hold, what will you need to put down on the property? Lender policies vary, but you should expect most lenders to require higher down payments from investor than from owner-occupied housing. How will the amount of cash required affect your personal budget and your investment portfolio?

5. *How long will it be necessary to hold the property?* Finally, you need to identify the likely time frame for your long-term hold. If you believe you will be able to sell at a profit within one year, set that goal for yourself. However, you might also conclude that there are good reasons to hold converted properties longer than originally planned. You enjoy a significant tax advantage by holding rental property, and you are allowed to deduct up to $25,000 in annual net losses. With most other investments that might generate a *passive loss,* you are not allowed to deduct those losses but must apply them against passive gains in future years. If you hold investment property more than one year, you are taxed at favorable *long-term capital gains* rates. In addition, if property values are rising, it may be more profitable to hold properties and make a higher profit later on.

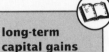

long-term capital gains

any gains from investments that were held for 12 months or longer, which are taxed at lower rates than ordinary income or short-term capital gains (gains on investments owned for less than 12 months).

Cash Flow Risks and Solutions

Potential cash flow problems are easily overlooked or discounted by investors. Whether you employ a flipping strategy or a long-term hold, the most critical question is whether you will be able to afford negative cash flow if and when it occurs.

Consider a situation in which monthly negative cash flow offsets a gradual increase in property value. In this scenario, you are making no profit because you're spending additional money every month, and yet your budget suffers at the same time. You also risk exposure to other risks, such as discovery of the need for a major repair, a tenant not paying rent or destroying your property, or a catastrophic event not covered by insurance (such as flood, earthquake, or volcano damages).

The cash flow problem is only the beginning. Throughout a period of negative cash flow, you face additional risks *and* you have investment capital tied up in an illiquid investment. If this occurs, you need to decide whether you are better off getting out and cutting your losses, or figuring out a way to cure the cash flow problem. Possible solutions may include:

1. *Refinancing the mortgage.* You may be paying high interest because you needed to get a loan quickly, when a flipping strategy became a long-term rental. It may be worthwhile to shop for a better deal. Cash flow can be eased in one of two ways. First,

look for a lower interest rate; interest reduces by about $60 to $65 for each point of reduced interest per $100,000 loan balance (based on a 30-year loan).

The second way to ease cash flow is by refinancing for a longer repayment term. The longer the mortgage term is, the lower your monthly payments. Although overall interest will be higher with a longer term, the negative cash flow problem is short term, and you solve the short-term problem by extending the repayment period. A mortgage at 7 percent for $100,000 costs $230 less over 30 years than the same loan and rate for 15 years.

2. *Increasing rent.* It is not always possible to increase rent, especially if you're already charging market rates. But if your rent is too low, you may increase it. With this possibility in mind, if you are seeking a way to sell a converted property, rent it out on a month-to-month basis rather than through a lease.

3. *Selling an option to a tenant or prospective buyer.* You also increase cash flow by selling an option to buy the property. This may solve two problems. First, it can ease your month-to-month negative cash flow. (If the option is sold to a tenant, it is also less likely that tenant will vacate the property.) Second, if exercised, the option gives you a way out of the equity position. Thus, be sure the option's exercise price is adequate to make the position whole or, if possible, to produce a profit upon exercise.

4. *Swapping properties with another investor.* Some investors have been able to get out of an undesired ownership position by finding someone who wants an exchange. There may be any number of reasons that someone would be interested in acquiring a property even with negative cash flow. A prospective buyer is not necessarily an investor—however, he or she might want to buy a home in the specific neighborhood. By swapping your property for one with better cash flow, you may solve your problem by going through this transaction.

5. *Converting the investment to primary residence.* You may be facing a situation in which you would be willing to move into the rental property and convert your present home to a replacement rental. This makes sense when your house payments are low enough so that you will be able to produce positive cash flow, when the move makes sense based on investment value and appreciation,

and when the move is made for good reasons and not out of desperation (for example, merely due to the need to solve a cash flow problem).

Cash flow risk is more serious and potentially damaging than market risk itself. Investors tend to focus on price, with the idea that investing at today's price level will be profitable because values are rising in the area. Remember, if you cannot afford to make payments and keep up expenses on the property, the plan will not work out well.

In addition, cash flow problems tend to persist over time and are not likely to be cured by changes in the market. Depending on growing market rates for rentals as a solution is not advisable, because increases in market rates tend to occur gradually and over time, and there is always the possibility of declining rental demand, which would have the opposite effect—higher vacancies and lower rental rates.

The longer cash flow problems persist, the more erosion occurs in current and future profitability. Thus, even selling a property at an apparent profit (based on changes in actual market value), you need to evaluate the long-term negative impact of having to pay out cash each month just to support the property. If you earn a 10 percent return in three years, but you lose 4 to 5 percent each year, your true net will be a loss and not a profit.

For any conversion situation, the analysis of risk versus reward has to include a realistic study of cash flow and of the effects of negative cash flow on overall profits. The risk of the property flipping strategy is that the flip itself will be planned at a time when the market softens, so that profits will not be possible. At that time, your decision has to be based on cash flow prospects. If it looks like you will be able to cover cash flow for the next few months (even minimally), you might decide to carry the investment in the hope that prices will turn around within a year. But if you become convinced that cash flow is going to erode the profitability of the investment, you are better off selling at a loss and avoiding greater losses in the future.

Key Point

Negative cash flow is both a strain on your family's budget and a drain on future profits. You may be better off taking a small loss now and ending the negative cash flow as quickly as possible.

No one wants to accept losses. Like all investors, however, property flippers experience occasional losses. There are no guarantees of 100 percent success in any market. You can succeed by making a profit more often than a loss, and you will learn from your losses to make you wiser in the future.

The Capital and Credit Risk in Conversions

In addition to cash flow risks, conversion strategies may create two other types of risk worth analyzing. These are capital and credit risks.

Capital risk refers to the liquidity problem of long-term real estate investing. As long as you are required to make a down payment on investment property, some level of capital is tied up in the investment. If your lender requires a 30 percent down payment, a $200,000 property will need $60,000 in cash down payment. For most people this will represent a major drain on cash assets.

The more properties you keep in your portfolio as investments, the greater this capital risk becomes. In theory, you can use *built-up equity* in one property to finance the purchase of another and keep this idea rolling for an indefinite number of acquisitions. In practice, there will be a limit to the amount of built-up equity you can access through refinancing *and* in the amount of new loans that lenders will be willing to approve. If you try to build a real estate portfolio on highly leveraged funding, you eventually find that your own at-risk capital limits the number of properties you can purchase. For most people, having three or four properties in an investment portfolio is the maximum on the basis of net cash flow, investment capital, and lender policies.

built-up equity
the equity in real estate accumulated through growth in market value and, as a secondary source, in payments against outstanding mortgage loan balances.

Credit risk is equally limiting for investors. If you have too many properties in your long-term portfolio, lenders become nervous about your

---

Key Point

Most people have a relatively small amount of capital available for real estate investing. This limits the amount of leverage you can use—in spite of some get-rich-quick claims to the contrary.

> ### Key Point
>
> Credit risk is not simply the limitation on how much borrowing you are allowed to do. If you are overextended with investment real estate, you may not be able to get new credit, even when your history is excellent.

risk exposure. A change in local vacancy rates could jeopardize all of your loans. In addition, nonmortgage sources looking at your credit report may also become concerned when you have too much outstanding credit (which includes mortgage loans as well as other debts). So you may find your application for store revolving credit or for credit cards declined if you have too many mortgage loans outstanding.

So one aspect to credit risk is the limitation you place on yourself if you acquire too many leveraged properties. The other limitation is the loss of ability to gain additional credit. If you need to open a new account, the credit risk associated with owning investment property may work as an inhibiting factor.

The essential elements needed to make a conversion strategy successful include:

1. *Strong credit rating.* Real estate investors need excellent credit, without any doubt. If your credit is weak or poor, you will have great difficulty financing a conversion property. While homeowners have a relatively easy time finding a lender (even with poor credit, lenders will loan for owner-occupied properties rather liberally and at somewhat higher-than-average rates), investors may not enjoy the same ease of financing. The requirements are stricter and investors are often held to a higher qualification standard in terms of down payment, interest rate, and lender fees.

2. *Exceptional lender contacts.* It certainly helps for all property flipping strategies and long-term rental properties, if you have contact with a lender who knows you and who is willing and able to grant loans. This may be a conventional lender with flexibility in loan policies or, on the other end of the spectrum, a private lender who wants to invest in secured mortgages.

3. *Adequate property-specific cash flow.* No property investment can be justified if you will have to live with negative cash flow. Some would disagree with this statement, pointing out that in very strong

markets, it is possible to assume prices will outpace the negative cash flow—and that is sometimes true, but eventually the market changes and someone ends up losing a lot of money (or finding themselves holding property they cannot afford to keep and cannot afford to sell). The longer you hold properties with negative cash flow, the more that problem erodes your future profit.

4. *Flexibility in positioning of your assets.* If you use asset allocation formulas to define your ideal portfolio, be aware of how a conversion will distort your desired use of investment capital. If you are going to flip properties with the awareness that you may decide to convert a property to a long-term hold (for the negative reason of a weakened market or for the positive reason that prices continue to grow), you may need to employ a flexible investment strategy.

5. *Imaginative problem-solving alternatives.* Do not overlook the possibilities beyond holding or selling. Entering into a property exchange or swapping rental property with your primary residence are two possible alternatives. Refinancing to get lower rates or extend a repayment period also eases cash flow.

6. *A willingness to cut losses.* Not every investment decision will be profitable. Everyone has to accept losses from time to time. The truly wise investor recognizes that it is better to accept a small loss today than hold on too long and end up with a larger loss later.

7. *Realistic contingency planning.* In any strategy you use, always be aware of what the outcome is going to be in the worst-case scenario. Contingency planning should be designed to help you:

    a. Eliminate situations that are simply too high risk for you to pursue.
    b. Create the maximum profit outcome in the shortest possible time.
    c. Revise your profitability profile if you see greater opportunities through conversion.
    d. Minimize losses when the plan simply does not work, so that you do not end up with larger losses as a result of the mistake.

Whether you go into real estate primarily to speculate, to find long-term investments, or to combine both strategies, you look for value where it exists. The next chapter describes the ways that investors locate opportunities.

Locating Your Opportunities

Where to Find Values

Flipping properties is best accomplished on the basis of accurate, timely, and in-depth intelligence gathering. Investors should never jump into a plan without knowing the risks on every possible level.

The worst-case scenario described in the last chapter, as applied to contingency planning, is a smart way to manage risks and to strategize in advance to minimize losses if the market moves in an unexpected direction. In addition to contingency planning, it also makes sense to analyze the entire market thoroughly in order to become an expert on the local real estate market and know how to find value.

The difficulty in recognizing cycles while in the middle of them makes property flipping a matter of proper timing. Even this is an understatement when you consider that cyclical change is rarely experienced in a straight line. The economic models found in books and classrooms used to explain cyclical influences of supply and demand are not accurate. They usually demonstrate cause and effect via a series of gentle sloping lines. In reality, markets move and change chaotically and provide many false starts implying economic improvement in an otherwise downward trend—or a reversal of short duration within a strongly rising price market. This is important to keep in mind because you cannot rely on momentary change to judge the market; you need to perform regionally based analysis over a period of months.

> ### Key Point
>
> Knowledge truly is power in real estate (and in all types of investing). Knowing how to find value is the key to avoiding loss and to maximizing profit.

Rather than giving a lot of significance to the latest trends in real estate pricing and supply-and-demand factors, using a moving average tends to smooth out the chaotic month-to-month outcomes. So when you study the spread, time on the market, and current inventory of homes for sale, remember that the latest entry in a trend is not confirmation of a reversal (or even of a continuation in the existing trend). It is simply the latest entry in the ongoing trend.

While the statistical study of the housing market is useful and may provide valuable intelligence about today's market, it is only part of the equation. Of far greater importance is your own intimate knowledge of your local market, based on observation and your own examination of the city or town, neighborhoods, and single pieces of property.

magic thinking
a form of "casual reasoning" in which beliefs, unsupportable by science, replace reasoning. For example, people carry good luck tokens or wear "lucky" clothing. Applied to the mentally ill, magic thinking involves a belief in special power, such as the ability to wish someone dead. Applied to investors, magic thinking includes a belief that thinking the right thoughts may make an investment increase in value.

Secrets of Real Estate Bargains

Every investor, in every market, seeks out that elusive "sweet deal" that will be easy, fast, and incredibly profitable. Stock market investors more than most people are known for variations in *magic thinking* about stock values and incredible riches that may be had if only the secrets were discovered.

Using sound methods leads to finding real estate bargains, but there is nothing magic to it. All investment knowledge comes from research, and the better your research, the more likely you *will* find bargains. To research effectively, remember these guidelines:

Key Point
Finding bargains in real estate involves time and effort. If you want to get rich quick, property flipping probably is not the way to go.

1. *Use the statistical measurements of the market, but only as a starting point.* The major statistical measurements of the market—the spread, time on the market, and current inventory of homes for sale—are valuable indicators if studied as part of a longer-term trend (one full year, for example). But these data are only the starting points in what should be a more in-depth analysis of your local market.

2. *Put in a lot of "walking around" time.* The best way to become familiar with your local market is by getting out and looking at properties. Go to open houses, compare neighborhoods and values, and determine why some areas command higher prices for the same configuration of homes. See what kind of volume open houses get. Also check developments under construction, view models, and speak with developers' representatives. Are developers charging a lot for land and placing cheap manufacturer housing on the lots? Or are they providing exceptionally crafted homes at a premium? Every strategic approach to the market has its own effect on prices, but may affect different pricing levels in the larger picture.

3. *Talk to real estate agents, appraisers, assessors, lenders, contractors, and developers in your town.* Talk to everyone. All of the people working in real estate have a particular point of view, and collectively these add up to insights about the local market. The real estate agent's opinion may be at odds with lenders or developers. Once you understand each source's point of view, you will be better equipped to make informed judgments about the health of the market and the direction in which it is moving. Visit real estate offices and look over the current listings offered. If an agent will allow you to see the multiple listing service book (or better yet, the online version), you can gain a good comprehensive view of what is out there.

4. *Watch and study the want ads.* Read the daily paper as well as real estate magazines designed to provide listings. Remember, though,

that neither of these sources is the entire market. You need to put your own time into judging the overall picture. Assuming you are going to emphasize the housing market, it also pays to look over "for rent" ads as well as ads for raw land, commercial property, and multiple-unit housing (usually found in the "investment property" section of the want ads).

5. *Compare your local market to markets in nearby areas. Judge the causes of property value growth relative to your own area.* Every area's real estate market changes due to predictable influences. If population is rising, housing will be needed and, if the rate of construction does not keep up with demand, prices will rise. Employment trends often predict housing prices. When employers come into an area (or leave), you can expect to see predictable changes in the market within a few months. Commute distance to nearby cities is another important factor. When prices get too high in a one-hour commute distance around a city, the predictable next step is for property values in a 90-minute commute range to begin climbing as well. Commuting workers will make a trade-off between affordable housing and commute time, and will be willing to spend more time traveling each day for lower housing costs.

Judging the *Region:* City, Town, or County

The task of valuation begins with a study of regional economic and market factors. It is a mistake to place too much value in national averages that are reported on the news. Averages are just that; they may set an overall tone to the market at large, but they reveal nothing about what is going on in your immediate region.

　　Just as the Dow Jones Industrial Average is an index of a few stocks and a widely used method for assessing the overall stock market, the national averages of home price trends, building starts, or first-time buyers

---

Key Point

Using averages in any market is dangerous because averages tell you nothing about a specific city or town. You need to emphasize and focus on regional trends.

reveal nothing of value to you. What actually counts is what is going on in your city, town, or county. A lot of time is spent worrying about real estate bubbles, but the regional nature of real estate should be reassuring. A bubble is not likely to burst everywhere at the same time; however, because of the national emphasis in the news, it is easy to assume that this will be the case.

It is more likely that when real estate bubbles do burst, it will occur in very specific regional markets. Those areas where prices have risen most dramatically are most vulnerable to that outcome, especially when price increases have been caused largely by speculation (including property flipping). In those areas, prices may be increasing at unbelievable rates but are inevitably going to crash one day.

However, in any regional market, specific conditions are going to vary considerably. Some of the more important factors affecting regional value—and you may note that *all* of these influences are regional in nature—include:

1. *Employment trends.* Demand for housing often is defined by employment more than by any other factors. If the jobs are there, people stay, and if jobs increase, new families move to the area. Whenever demand exceeds supply of housing, prices rise, often dramatically and quickly.

2. *Demographic trends.* In addition to employment trends, population grows or declines for numerous reasons. Some cities are desirable retirement centers due to recreation, climate, low crime, and housing prices. For example, central Florida became a center for retirement living during the 1990s when large-scale retirement communities combining housing, golf, and shopping outlets were designed and built. The Villages is one nationally known example. Retirement populations are also drawn to warm and dry climates such as those of the Phoenix area. There, housing has been affordable, and communities became dominated by self-contained gated communities, which include their own recreation, shopping centers, and even on-site medical care.

3. *Commute distance to large cities.* A pattern emerges as populations in urban centers increase. Property values rise when housing demand forces families out farther from the city center. It may be acceptable to commute for one hour or less within a range of housing prices; but when prices exceed that level, people have to

make a choice: pay more for housing or move farther from the city and accept a longer commute. This pattern has been witnessed in many cities, including Washington, D.C., New York, Los Angeles, Chicago, and San Francisco, to name a few. Expanded commutes become affordable compared to housing that once cost about $125,000 having grown to prices well above a half million, which has occurred in the bedroom communities of all of these metropolitan areas. Commuting patterns and price trends become a dependable gauge of housing price trends. And it can be measured. In San Francisco and the expensive communities to the immediate north (across the Golden Gate Bridge in Marin County) housing prices were consistently about $10,000 *per mile* as one moved closer to the city. So a house in San Rafael, California, might have sold for $300,000 in 1991 and a similar house 35 miles to the south (and right at the bridge) in Sausalito would be $650,000 − 35 miles × $10,000 = $350,000 ... and $350,000 + $300,000 = $650.000. The same level of change will not apply everywhere and this is an extreme example. It demonstrates how commute distance affects housing prices.

4. *Nearby attractions.* Prices are also affected by proximity to recreation, transportation, entertainment, and tourism-related attractions. So properties near major theme parks, bus or train stations, golf courses, or well-known landmarks are likely to command a premium in market value. Two properties of a similar size, age, and character will be priced in vastly different ranges based on these attributes. A house next to a golf course or a park will be priced above one far removed from these amenities.

Neighborhood Valuation

The overall regional characteristics that determine value can be even more finely observed when you get down to the neighborhood level. Here, specific features—age, condition, crime levels, very local amenities,

---

Key Point

Values change for specific reasons and do not simply happen. By knowing the causes as well as the effects, you will be better situated to recognize emerging opportunities before most others.

and population levels—define how neighborhood values change over time.

A series of market factors directly affects how value develops and how the trends in prices actually occur. Most people have heard of *supply and demand,* but you will observe that within a market, certain properties seem to respond not to the classic economic cycle, but to other factors. Under the definition of supply and demand, which is a useful theory to use as a starting point in determining value, all commodities should react to predictable market forces. High supply causes lower prices, and higher demand causes higher prices. This is true as a general rule, but there is more to valuation.

The supply and demand cycle may also be thought of as the course of a trend, but actual neighborhood price trend (as well as prices of individual properties) are subject to the *ten valuation principles.* These are:

1. *Anticipation.* The tendency of markets (in general as well as in real estate) to experience trend patterns based on the expectation of future events. Fears of a real estate bubble bursting may bring prices down, or the belief that future prices will rise may itself causes higher prices.

2. *Change.* The fact that nothing remains the same as it is today makes the point that future real estate values are going to be based on new conditions, supply and demand, economic factors, and both expected and unexpected events.

3. *Competition.* The impact of competing forces on real estate values refers both to competition among investors and to land use itself. A limited supply of land and its final use determine valuation; when land is scarce, prices are driven up, and when investors want specific types of land or property, that also drives up prices.

supply and demand
the market forces at work that control and create cyclical price changes and, to a degree, value of property. Growing supply causes prices to fall and growing demand causes prices to rise.

ten valuation principles
the rules governing the ways that value of real estate evolves: anticipation, change, competition, conformity, contribution, highest and best use, plottage, progression, regression, and substitution.

anticipation
the tendency of markets to demonstrate price trends due to the expectation of future events or changes.

competition

the economic driving force creating growth or decline in market value of property. Greater competition for scarcer land drives prices up, and a lack of interest (low competition) in a type of property brings prices down.

conformity

a principle of valuation; properties similar in size, age, condition, numbers of rooms, and amount of land tend to change in price in a uniform manner. Properties that do not conform to typical properties in the same area will not grow at the same rate as conforming properties.

contribution

the principle stating that improvements add value as a factor of supply and demand, and not based on actual cost of those improvements.

4. *Conformity.* This factor reveals that when houses in a neighborhood are improved beyond the *typical* configuration (or when the size, age, or condition of properties is not in conformity) the market value will be inhibited. The value of overimproved (nonconforming) properties will not be likely to grow beyond the growth of conforming properties.

5. *Contribution.* This valuation concept states that improvements to property add value, but only as part of the supply-and-demand cycle. Improvements do not necessarily add value based on actual cost. For example, a remodel job adds value to a house when prices are rising, but it may add little or no value when prices are flat or falling.

6. *Highest and best use.* A principle often cited by appraisers is this one—the observation that real estate value is going to be at the maximum when it is used in the best way available, given its features, location, topography, and access.

7. *Plottage.* This concept refers to order; when land is zoned similarly and put to the same use, it tends to be more valuable. In comparison, random and unzoned usage, dissimilar lot size and shape, and inconsistent zoning tends to hold values down.

8. *Progression.* This principle states that a property's value is likely to increase when other properties located nearby are newer, in better condition, or built with better materials. The idea of progression is that a property benefits when other, similar properties are improved. This concept is also expressed in the maxim for real estate investors: "Buy the worst house on a good block."

9. *Regression.* The opposite of progression is regression, the observation that a property's value is likely to decline when other nearby properties are in disrepair, in poorer condition, or not being as well cared for.

10. *Substitution.* This concept is very similar to conformity, but not exactly. Substitution is the principle that growth in property value will be limited by the market value of similar properties in the same neighborhood or in similar areas. Appraisers seek *comparable properties* as a means for setting value during an appraisal, and then adjust the subject property's value based on age, condition, size, and features.

highest and best use
a principle of valuation, stating that real estate values are at a maximum when land is used in the most effective manner possible, given its features.

The Transition Factor

Property flippers are investors who are able to recognize bargains. However, bargains tend to last only a short time. Deep discounts in property value are rare and do not last long; and these often depend on one of three current market factors:

plottage
the principle of valuation stating that uniformity in land zoning and use tends to hold and increase value, and inconsistent zoning and planning tends to adversely impact values.

1. *A distressed situation.* The most likely source for consistent property flipping opportunities is distressed properties. These can be located through lenders in most instances. A lender wanting to get out of deals where properties are in default have a choice. They must take possession of the property, fix any problems, and then sell it or find someone to take the property off their hands. It often means homes with little market-level equity involved, so lenders need to offer a discount in order to attract investors. And when additional money has to be spent to fix problems with the property, the lender may even take a loss on the deal just to be rid of the obligation.

progression
the observation that a property's market value is likely to increase when it is located near similar properties of higher quality and whose market value is increasing.

regression

a valuation principle stating that a property's value may decline if and when other, similar properties in the same area are falling in value.

substitution

the principle stating that a property's value and potential growth will be limited to the same factors in other, similar properties in the same or similar neighborhoods.

comparable properties

in appraisal, properties that are found in the same neighborhood or in similar neighborhoods and sharing the same features as a property being appraised.

The foreclosure market is a good source to find property flipping deals. But you may also find them in cases where people are going through divorce, settling the estate of a deceased relative, or having trouble with tenants.

2. *A highly speculative market environment.* A high-risk market is one where property values are climbing dramatically and in a relatively short period of time. It is possible to accomplish a rapid turnaround in a property flip; but such markets may often depend on finding someone else trying to do the same thing. Eventually, new speculators dry up and if property flipping speculation is driving the market, the risks are considerable. In the early 2000s, the Florida market for condominiums was typical of this situation. The market was originally driven by ever-growing retirement demand for condos. As the market heated up, however, it became more speculative. Condo units in developments could be purchased while still in the planning stage— and the same units could be sold for a considerable profit before construction was complete!

The question worth asking in markets such as this is: What is driving the demand and how long will that last? If the "greed factor" is in play, meaning that speculation is driving prices up but real demand no longer exists, then you have to expect the bubble to burst at some point. Then you have to also realize that someone will be stuck with all of those units, because demand is not there. So the bargain may be an illusion, and the opportunity is really a matter of timing and luck.

Key Point

Exceptional opportunities are exciting, especially if it is possible to create short-term but highly profitable flips. But do not forget that the greater the opportunity, the greater the risk.

Key Point

Remember, "distressed" properties usually involve distressed people. This does not mean you need to take advantage in order to profit. As a property flipper, you can structure deals to solve the problems encountered by the unfortunate homeowner who is in over his or her head. A property flipper can also relieve the lender of a defaulted mortgage and turn the venture into a profitable property flip as well.

3. *Locating a private deal with a motivated seller.* You can find nicely discounted properties working directly with sellers. If they want to sell quickly and do not want to pay real estate commissions, they may also offer a nice discount. You are not likely to find such deals through real estate agents. Why should an agent list a property being offered at a discount? They may buy such properties for themselves and make the profit, or work as dealers to match the seller with a willing buyer. In that case, the agent may earn a commission *and* make a profit on the transaction. So you are not going to find discounted properties among publicly listed properties.

The deeply discounted property is likely to be located in a neighborhood going through either a *positive transition* or a *negative transition*. In the first instance, previously outdated or poorly maintained homes are being revitalized or even taken down and replaced with more modern buildings. Vacant lots are being purchased and new buildings are going up. Crime rates are declining as families move into the area. A city may improve infrastructure as property values (and tax revenues) rise.

positive transition

a change in a neighborhood in which values are increasing due to renovation of existing homes, replacement of outdated properties, and other favorable change.

Key Point

Finding a motivated seller is a great opportunity. Look at every deal critically and be sure you know the reasons the seller is motivated. Avoid buying someone else's problem because at some point you give up being the buyer and become the seller.

A neighborhood going through a negative transition experiences the opposite trend. Property values are falling because properties are outdated and uncared for, and the situation is getting worse. Houses are abandoned, crime is on the rise, and properties remain for sale without market interest for many months.

negative transition

a change in neighborhoods in which properties are empty or abandoned, crime is rising, and property values are falling due to lack of care, high rates of absentee ownership, or other negative trends.

Transitions offer property flipping opportunities. If you recognize early signs of an emerging positive transition, you may find low-priced properties that are likely to grow in value over a short period of time (months rather than years). Buying into a positive transition is usually a profitable strategy.

A more difficult strategy (but potentially just as profitable) is to buy very low-priced properties in neighborhoods at the bottom of the value barrel. Once an area's value has declined to the point that no one else wants to buy, prices will be as low as they can get. At such times, you may employ a number of strategies. Simply buying properties and renting them out to wait out the market is the most obvious of these, but is potentially problematic in the short term. For example, higher vacancies are always a possibility in troubled areas, not to mention the constant threat of high crime levels, vandalism, arson, and other dangers that will hold property values down at least in the immediate future.

A second strategy is to purchase a number of properties consisting of small houses, vacant lots, or lots with mobile homes; bundle these together, and sell as a single unit. This is a complex transaction involving locating a buyer interested in investing in a depressed area. A developer or contractor (who may also recognize that the neighborhood will eventually improve) might be willing to purchase bundled properties and develop them over time or work with tenants. One way to do this is to offer

---

Key Point

Because positive transition is relatively easy for making money in real estate, almost every property flipper, speculator, and long-term investor wants to find such a market. This means there will be fewer exceptional deals to go around.

Key Point

Working in the depressed neighborhood is more difficult for property flipping, but potentially more profitable. As long as you understand the range of problems you must deal with, this may be a viable alternative to the more popular positive transition area.

---

tenants a type of lease option, including the condition that delinquent lease payments negate the entire option. In this sort of transaction, tenants eventually buy the property or it is turned over two or more times with new tenants. This type of dealing is very stressful, and an owner in such an area will have to deal continuously with tenants late with rent payments, properties that are run-down or vandalized, and the ever-present need to evict people who simply do not cooperate. Another risk is that of becoming a slumlord, literally. If the margins for profit are too slim, it becomes ever more difficult to justify performing needed repairs. Even people with good intentions may find themselves in a no-win situation.

A more rewarding way to invest in transitional neighborhoods is to locate properties where values are already on the rise. For example, in the San Francisco Bay Area, where median housing prices are close to $800,000, families are constantly looking for lower-than-market places to live. If they cannot find bargains, they often leave the area. In such an inflated price market, property flipping is possible, but with an extra zero added (so you can flip $800,000 properties rather than $80,000 ones). This requires higher levels of investment, greater market risk, and oftentimes fewer opportunities.

In one neighborhood, a couple found a house in an overlooked neighborhood called Sunnyside, for $600,000. A bargain? Yes, considering that homes in the neighborhood usually sell for $700,000 and up as of 2006 (and with predictions that within a year or two properties will be impossible to find under $1 million).

Due to these price trends, neighborhoods that were once typified by families with children have become centers for two-income, young professionals whose careers preclude starting a family. In San Francisco's Sunnyside, a 10-year analysis (1990 to 2000) by San Francisco State University revealed a decline of about 20 percent in families with children. The city's overall population of children had declined over a 14-year period (through 2004) by 7,000. The city now has the fewest children per capita of any major U.S. city. These outcomes can be traced specifically to dramatically rising housing prices, which one-income families with children simply cannot afford.[1]

Attributes of Strong Real Estate Markets

Neighborhoods in transition—like the Sunnyside in San Francisco—are not always suitable candidates for property flipping. Another sort of "transition" has taken place over the past two decades in areas like Florida and Arizona, which have experienced a migration of retirees.

In these areas, where climate and affordability are major factors, the transition has gone from slow-growth or no-growth environments based on lack of jobs, to high-growth transitional environments based on increasing retirement populations.

This is more of a cultural transition than a neighborhood transition or at the very least a transition in which a "neighborhood" is more properly and accurately defined as an entire community. In many cases, those communities simply did not exist 20 years ago but were built out of nothing. Many self-contained neighborhoods are so massive that they incorporate as new cities, and include gated residential areas, shopping centers, newly built hospitals, and utility companies, all within the new "neighborhood." Examples include The Villages and Celebration, Florida, and dozens of similar projects in Phoenix, Scottsdale, and Chandler, Arizona. The appeal of combining residential living at affordable price levels with recreational facilities on site (usually large golf courses, tennis, swimming, and biking) is a transitional trend that is going to accelerate over the next few years as the Baby Boomers begin retiring in massive numbers.

These trends in migratory retirement living may present many different kinds of opportunities. Property flipping is likely to occur during

---

Key Point

A "transition" is not always limited to specific neighborhood attributes. It could also apply to and be caused by longer-term or more sweeping demographic and economic trends.

---

[1] Stacy Finz, "Fortune Shines on Sunnyside," *San Francisco Chronicle*, 20 November 2005.

construction phases and even be limited to speculation in raw land. But anticipating these trends in residential development may require longer-term investing, and are not always appropriate for most property flipping. Investing in these areas may require several years rather than a matter of weeks or months to become profitable.

To identify the "perfect" property flipping opportunity based on specific neighborhoods or houses, look for these signs:

1. *Activity in an area is picking up.* The trend is unmistakable when you see a growing level of activity. This can be measured in many ways, including more "for sale" signs going up, faster sales, and even an increase in the number of active real estate salespeople in the area.

2. *Housing prices are rising around the region due to growing demand.* The strong market, one in which housing prices are exceeding inflation, is the most appealing of all areas. Remember, however, that when housing does exceed inflation, it is not going to last forever.

3. *Secondary causes such as growing employment or transportation, are contributing to higher demand for housing.* Areas often become strong in terms of real estate demand due to changes beyond the number of homes or historical prices. If a major employer moves to the area or a new freeway passes close by, these events are likely to place greater demand on the local market. Of course, if employment is falling or an existing highway going through town is replaced by a bypass freeway, you can expect the opposite to occur in property values.

4. *Relatively few properties are on the market, compared to the past.* Contrary to the apparent trend of more properties going on the market, a positive transition can be seen in fewer properties going up for sale. This may occur because current owners anticipate that the market will rise in the near future, so they are waiting for

that to occur. It may also be the case that properties are selling faster, so that the "scarcity" is really the result of fast turnaround.

5. *Rather than sales closing below asked prices, many sales are big up above that level.* The market is often judged by analyzing the spread between asked price and final sales price. Typically, in moderately strong markets, final sales will run from 90 to 95 percent of asked prices. In weak markets, the spread is increasing lower (and even accompanied by a growing number of properties placed for sale and ultimately withdrawn without any acceptable offers). In exceptionally strong markets, sale prices actually exceed asked prices—not in every case, but in a growing number. So if buying demand is so strong that people are willing to offer more than the seller is asking, that is an exceptionally good sign that prices are moving upward strongly. In this instance, the price trend is established by demand trends rather than the more traditional dominance of supply within the market.

6. *You are able to locate houses for sale well below the going rate.* Even in markets with exceptionally high price levels or trends under way, you will continue to seek the exceptional bargain. Such a bargain comes about for numerous reasons, and it is often a matter of thorough scouting to find areas and specific properties meeting the criteria making property flipping viable. It is even possible in some markets that you simply will not be able to locate opportunities, and you will then need to look elsewhere.

The next chapter takes a more in-depth look at the methods used to set real estate values—and how valuation trends affect your ability to find property flipping opportunities.

7

Cost and Profit
What It Costs, What You Earn

S ome confusion exists over exactly how to compute your real estate net profit. There are many definitions of net profit, such as total return, net return, rate of return, and margin of profit, that mean essentially the same thing. A distinction, however, should be made between net profit and cash-based profit.

Figuring the Profit

There is a clear difference between net profit and cash-based profit. Net profit is the difference between adjusted purchase price and adjusted sales price expressed as a percentage. To calculate, divide the difference between the two dollar values by the adjusted purchase price:

$$\frac{\text{Adjusted sales price} - \text{Adjusted purchase price}}{\text{Adjusted purchase price}} = \text{Net profit}$$

For example, a property is originally purchased for an adjusted purchase price of $126,807 and is later sold for an adjusted sales price of $152,008. Net profit is:

$$\frac{\$152,008 - \$126,807}{\$126,807} = 19.9\%$$

115

Net profit is easily calculated, as demonstrated. To make profits truly comparable between two or more properties (or to compare actual outcome to your goals), you need to take one more step. You need to annualize the return, which means it has to be expressed as though the property were owned for exactly one year.

Returning to the previous example, if you had owned the property for exactly 12 months, then the 19.9 percent return represents an accurate annual outcome. If you had owned the property for only two months, the annualized return is considerably higher. To compute, divide the net profit by the number of months the property was owned and then multiply by 12 (months):

$$\frac{19.9}{2} \times 12 = 119.4\%$$

A word of caution about annualizing: It may be unrealistic to claim that you are able to earn 119.4 percent from property flipping. Such an outcome would be quite difficult to reproduce. The purpose in annualizing is to create an accurate and consistent means for comparison of outcomes. The adjustment can also work to reduce the net return upon annualization. For example, if you had owned a property for 15 months before earning 19.9 percent, annualized return would be:

$$\frac{19.9}{15} \times 12 = 15.9\%$$

In this outcome, a considerably lower annualized return resulted. This makes the point concerning net return: The simple calculation itself can distort outcomes if you do not also consider the time factor. The more quickly you turn over properties, the higher the annualized yield. Additionally, the longer you hold properties, the lower the annualized yield.

Key Point

The calculation of *profit* is more complex than simply multiplying a purchase price by a preconceived percentage. The calculation has to take much more into consideration.

The second type of return calculation is cash-based profit. This is a more reliable basis for judging results because it uses the actual cash you place at risk in a transaction. If you are able to flip a property without investing any cash whatsoever, this calculation is not useful. If you match up a seller and a buyer during escrow and go through the process making your profit as a dealer, this usually means you do not have any cash in play. For this reason, it is sensible to make both types of calculations. In any transaction in which you place money as a down payment, you can calculate cash-based profit in a property flipping transaction.

Returning once more to the previous example, net profit was calculated by comparing dollar amounts of the property transaction:

$$\frac{\$152,008 - \$126,807}{\$126,807} = 19.9\%$$

To calculate cash-based profit, the difference is divided by a different number—the actual amount of cash you place at risk. You would assume in this calculation that the property flip takes place quickly, so that you do not also have to calculate ongoing cash outlays as you would in the case of a long-term hold.

To adjust the calculation: Assuming the property's price (before closing adjustments) was $123,900 and you made a 30 percent down payment, your cash at risk would be:

$$\$123,900 \times 30\% = \$37,170$$

The cash-based return on this investment is:

$$\frac{\$152,008 - \$126,807}{\$37,170} = 67.8\%$$

As with all such calculations, the annualized version of this return will be considerably different than the calculation above. Like all types of annualized returns, the purpose is not to inaccurately indicate that an annualized return in double or triple digits is possible; its purpose is to develop a consistent means for comparison between the outcomes for two or more property investments.

Calculating Your Buyer's Closing Costs

The actual closing costs paid by buyer and seller vary by state and region. For example, in some states, sellers pay excise tax based on the sales price. So if the seller's closing costs are 9 percent of the sales price, an additional 2 percent excise tax will take that total up to 11 percent. Because of these kinds of variables, it is not reliable to try and estimate *all* closing costs on a percentage basis.

good-faith estimate
an estimate of a buyer's financing-related closing costs, required by the Real Estate Procedures Closing Act (RESPA).

RESPA
acronym for the Real Estate Procedures Closing Act, a federal law that requires lenders to provide borrowers with a good-faith estimate of loan costs.

Lenders are required to provide both buyers with a *good-faith estimate* of expenses due at closing related to the loan, which is usually the largest closing expense involved. This estimate is also called the *RESPA* good-faith estimate because it is required by the Real Estate Procedures Closing Act.

You can use percentages as a rough estimate once you know the rules in your state, and once you have been through a few closings. Of course, every deal will be different based on financing terms (for buyers), any inspection fees or the cost of repairs (for both buyer and seller), and any allowances granted by the seller to the buyer. (One way to deal with required work is to make the repair, and another is to include an allowance in the deal.)

To begin calculating your buyer's closing costs, make a list of potential sources for those costs, and then complete a buyer's closing worksheet.

The worksheet should include—at the very least—the following:

1. *Financing closing costs.* For buyers, the most expensive closing costs are usually those related to getting a loan. A *loan origination fee* is a fancy term for *points*, usually representing a percentage of the amount borrowed. One point is one percent; so if you are borrowing $80,000 and the lender wants two points, that means you pay $1,600 at closing.

    A variation on points that you might be able to negotiate with the lender is called a *loan discount* or *discount point*. You agree to pay the loan discount in exchange for a reduced interest rate. (Each point normally reduces the loan's interest rate by 1/8th of a percentage point.) But if you plan to flip the property and not hold it for the long term, loan discounts are probably not worth the cost. If you are going to keep the property for several years, it is worth calculating the difference a loan discount makes.

    The borrower will also be required to pay a property appraisal fee. This fee varies depending on whether the lender sends out their own employee to look at the property or hires an independent appraiser. Remember, if you are paying the fee you are also entitled to a copy of the appraisal report. This is a valuable document if you plan to flip the property in less than six months. The appraisal might note that the house is in disrepair and the kitchen is obsolete.

loan origination fee

a charge by lenders, also called *points*, to cover the cost of processing the loan. Each point is usually equal to 1 percent of the amount being borrowed.

points

charges by lenders for processing a mortgage loan. A point is equal to 1 percent of the amount being borrowed and is charged to the buyer.

loan discount

a charge lenders assess to borrowers in exchange for a reduced interest rate on a mortgage loan; also called a *discount point*.

discount point

a loan discount; a point charged in exchange for a reduced rate on a mortgage loan.

mortgage insurance

a type of insurance charged by lenders to borrowers when down payment level is less than 20 percent of the purchase price. This policy protects the lender in case of default on the loan.

prepaid expenses

certain expenses required to be paid in advance by buyers, charged in escrow. For example, any insurance premiums will be charged in advance.

If you repair the flaws and upgrade the kitchen, that could help bolster the price and the appraisal will support matching the house to higher-priced comparables, or "comps" as appraisers refer to the properties used in their reports.

As the borrower, you will also be required to pay any inspection fees not paid by the seller, and a number of smaller fees: credit report fee and document filing fees, for example. You may also be charged an application fee if the lender requires you to carry *mortgage insurance*. This is required when your down payment is less than 20 percent of the sales price, and you are required to make monthly premium payments to protect the lender in case of default. (This should not be confused with mortgage life insurance, which is a life policy with a death benefit equal to the mortgage balance.)

2. *Prepaid expenses and prorated charges.* A second form of buyer's closing costs involves *prepaid expenses* and charges called *prorated expenses*. For example, you will probably be required to prepay fire and casualty insurance (six months' to one year's premium) and lenders will also calculate interest from closing date to the first due date of your loan payment. Prorations are your share of ongoing expenses. This usually includes utilities and property taxes. For example, a utility bill may cover 31 days and closing takes place 10 days before the due date. If the seller paid the previous bill, you will be prorated 10 days worth of the bill. And if a property tax bill covers 180 days and your closing takes place 30 days into the period, a seller's prepaid bill will be prorated, with 150 days prorated to you. Prorations can also work in reverse,

---

Key Point

Prepaid and prorated expenses are simply a methodical way of assigning ongoing expenses between buyer and seller.

with the seller charged and buyer credited for expenses that are due but not yet paid.

3. *Escrow expenses.* A third area where buyers may be required to pay involves escrow-related charges. An escrow company or attorney handling the closing process has to be paid, and an escrow fee is assessed to buyer and seller. This covers not only the fee for the escrow agent, but any required notary, recording, and filing fees paid through the escrow account.

4. *Other fees.* Finally, you will have to pay for inspections you ask for as part of your offer. These include a home inspection and any specialized inspections such as one for termites and other pests. If you purchase a home warranty, the premium for that will also be collected during escrow. You are also required to pay for a *title search*, a process of checking recordings to ensure that no undisclosed liens or mortgages have been filed against the property. For example, if the seller lost a lawsuit but never made a court-ordered payment, the winning side may file a lien against the property. The title search is undertaken to discover undisclosed liens, so the seller can pay them during escrow. Because some liens may be missed in the title search, you are also required to buy a title insurance policy. A one-time premium is charged during escrow.

If the property you are buying is in a condo or co-op development, you might be required to pay additional charges, such as a one-time *impact fee* or *transfer fee.* In such situations, you will also be prorated annual association fees or dues.

A summary worksheet of buyer's closing costs is shown in Figure 7-1.

prorated expenses

any expenses shared between seller and buyer, with the total divided based on the number of days in the liability period.

title search

a closing cost charged to the buyer, involving checking the county records for any undisclosed liens, mortgages, or judgments against the property.

impact fee

a fee charged to buyers when the property is part of a condo or co-op development; also called a transfer fee.

transfer fee

another term for the impact fee charged to buyers in condo or co-op developments.

Buyer's Closing Costs

Worksheet

Lender fees:

       Loan origination fees   _____

       Loan discount fee   _____

       Appraisal fee   _____

       Credit report fee   _____

       Mortgage insurance application   _____

       Other fees _____   _____

Prepaid and prorated expenses:

       Interest   _____

       Insurance   _____

       Rent   _____

       Property taxes   _____

       Utilities   _____

       Other fees _____   _____

Escrow fees:

       Escrow account fees   _____

Other fees:

       Inspections   _____

       Warranties   _____

       Title search   _____

       Title insurance   _____

       Other fees _____   _____

Estimated total buyer's closing costs

                                               _____

FIGURE 7.1 Buyer's Closing Costs

Estimating Your Seller's Closing Costs

The buyer and seller pay a vastly different range of closing costs, by type as well as by source. Your seller's closing costs include:

1. *Real estate commission.* The "standard" 6 percent commission is sometimes pushed up to 7 percent, but can be negotiated significantly lower, even down to 3 or 4 percent. There is no set rule. A common practice is to agree to a 6 percent commission on the first $100,000 and 3 percent above. On very high-priced properties, a ceiling may also be applied. However the agreement is structured, you should shop and compare rates before agreeing to any commission schedule; and you should also tie in speed of sale to the rate, so that the agent has an incentive to put your property at the top of the list.

2. *Seller's prepaid and prorated expenses.* Just as the buyer is prorated or precharged for some types of expenses, so is the seller. If the seller has prepaid an expense that belongs partially to the buyer, then the buyer is charged the correct amount and the seller is credited. The same applies in reverse: If a payment is due and not yet made, the seller is charged and the buyer is credited.

3. *Inspection fees and cost of repairs.* As seller, you might be required to pay for some inspections. You may have an advantage in agreeing to pay for inspections, on the premise that the inspector is aware of which side pays the bills. When an advocate for the buyer, the incentive may be to find things in need of repair; when working for the seller, the inspector might be less inclined to list minor items on a report.

4. *Appraisal fee.* In some instances, you may be smart to pay for an appraisal as part of your preparation to sell the property. By getting your own updated appraisal report, you save the buyer money (for the inspection) and you produce a document showing

---

Key Point

The real estate commission is normally the largest closing cost for the seller. But it can be mitigated through negotiation.

that the house is worth what you are asking (or possibly even worth more).

5. *Document, recording, escrow, and filing fees.* Sellers are required to pay various minor fees to record the sale and for the cost of going through escrow. If your state charges sellers an excise tax upon sale, this is also charged in escrow.

settlement statement

a document summarizing the entire real estate transaction and showing all exchanges of funds and payments between buyer and seller.

A summary of the seller's closing costs is included in the worksheet in Figure 7.2.

Both buyer and seller receive a *settlement statement*, a summary usually prepared by the escrow agent for both sides. It summarizes all exchanges of funds and concludes with the amount of cash paid to the seller or required to be deposited by the buyer.

A sample of the standardized form provided by HUDCLIPS, the HUD Client Information and Policy System, used for settlement statements is shown in Figure 7.3.

Estimating Your Net Basis

A property flip has to be planned out and profits have to be estimated based on your *net* profit. And this is most accurately computed based on actual difference in cash-in and cash-out totals.

The calculation of net adjusted purchase and sales prices explained earlier in this chapter involves taking into account all of the closing costs on both sides of the transaction. This is where it helps if you are able to pin down a very accurate percentage. This helps you to know exactly what you need to achieve in order to make a profit.

Key Point
Even when you know with a degree of accuracy what your closing costs will be, some work will be required to figure out how much to sell properties for, to achieve your goal.

Seller's Closing Costs

Worksheet

Real estate commission   _____

Prepaid and prorated expenses:

      Taxes   _____
      Utilities   _____
      Other _____   _____

Inspection fee and cost of repairs:

      Inspections   _____
      Repairs   _____
      Other _____   _____

Appraisal fee   _____

Other fees:

      Document   _____
      Recording   _____
      Escrow   _____
      Filing   _____
      Excise tax   _____

Total seller's closing costs   _____

FIGURE 7.2 Seller's Closing Costs

A. **Settlement Statement**　　U.S. Department of Housing and Urban Development　　OMB Approval No. 2502-0265 (expires 9/30/2006)

B. Type of Loan

1. ☐ FHA　2. ☐ FmHA　3. ☐ Conv. Unins. 4. ☐ VA　5. ☐ Conv. Ins.	6. File Number:	7. Loan Number:	8. Mortgage Insurance Case Number:

C. Note: This form is furnished to give you a statement of actual settlement costs. Amounts paid to and by the settlement agent are shown. Items marked "(p.o.c.)" were paid outside the closing; they are shown here for informational purposes and are not included in the totals.

D. Name & Address of Borrower:	E. Name & Address of Seller:	F. Name & Address of Lender:

G. Property Location:

H. Settlement Agent:	
Place of Settlement:	I. Settlement Date:

J. Summary of Borrower's Transaction		K. Summary of Seller's Transaction	
100. Gross Amount Due From Borrower		**400. Gross Amount Due To Seller**	
101. Contract sales price		401. Contract sales price	
102. Personal property		402. Personal property	
103. Settlement charges to borrower (line 1400)		403.	
104.		404.	
105.		405.	
Adjustments for items paid by seller in advance		**Adjustments for items paid by seller in advance**	
106. City/town taxes　　to		406. City/town taxes　　to	
107. County taxes　　to		407. County taxes　　to	
108. Assessments　　to		408. Assessments　　to	
109.		409.	
110.		410.	
111.		411.	
112.		412.	
120. Gross Amount Due From Borrower		**420. Gross Amount Due To Seller**	
200. Amounts Paid By Or In Behalf Of Borrower		**500. Reductions In Amount Due To Seller**	
201. Deposit or earnest money		501. Excess deposit (see instructions)	
202. Principal amount of new loan(s)		502. Settlement charges to seller (line 1400)	
203. Existing loan(s) taken subject to		503. Existing loan(s) taken subject to	
204.		504. Payoff of first mortgage loan	
205.		505. Payoff of second mortgage loan	
206.		506.	
207.		507.	
208.		508.	
209.		509.	
Adjustments for items unpaid by seller		**Adjustments for items unpaid by seller**	
210. City/town taxes　　to		510. City/town taxes　　to	
211. County taxes　　to		511. County taxes　　to	
212. Assessments　　to		512. Assessments　　to	
213.		513.	
214.		514.	
215.		515.	
216.		516.	
217.		517.	
218.		518.	
219.		519.	
220. Total Paid By/For Borrower		**520. Total Reduction Amount Due Seller**	
300. Cash At Settlement From/To Borrower		**600. Cash At Settlement To/From Seller**	
301. Gross Amount due from borrower (line 120)		601. Gross amount due to seller (line 420)	
302. Less amounts paid by/for borrower (line 220)	( )	602. Less reductions in amt. due seller (line 520)	( )
303. Cash ☐ From ☐ To Borrower		**603. Cash** ☐ To ☐ From Seller	

Section 5 of the Real Estate Settlement Procedures Act (RESPA) requires the following: • HUD must develop a Special Information Booklet to help persons borrowing money to finance the purchase of residential real estate to better understand the nature and costs of real estate settlement services; • Each lender must provide the booklet to all applicants from whom it receives or for whom it prepares a written application to borrow money to finance the purchase of residential real estate; • Lenders must prepare and distribute with the Booklet a Good Faith Estimate of the settlement costs that the borrower is likely to incur in connection with the settlement. These disclosures are mandatory.

Section 4(a) of RESPA mandates that HUD develop and prescribe this standard form to be used at the time of loan settlement to provide full disclosure of all charges imposed upon the borrower and seller. These are third party disclosures that are designed to provide the borrower with pertinent information during the settlement process in order to be a better shopper.

The Public Reporting Burden for this collection of information is estimated to average one hour per response, including the time for reviewing instructions, searching existing data sources, gathering and maintaining the data needed, and completing and reviewing the collection of information.

This agency may not collect this information, and you are not required to complete this form, unless it displays a currently valid OMB control number. The information requested does not lend itself to confidentiality.

FIGURE 7.3 HUDCLIPS Settlement Statement Form

L. Settlement Charges

700. Total Sales/Broker's Commission based on price $ @ % =		Paid From Borrowers Funds at Settlement	Paid From Seller's Funds at Settlement
Division of Commission (line 700) as follows:			
701. $ to			
702. $ to			
703. Commission paid at Settlement			
704.			
800. Items Payable In Connection With Loan			
801. Loan Origination Fee %			
802. Loan Discount %			
803. Appraisal Fee to			
804. Credit Report to			
805. Lender's Inspection Fee			
806. Mortgage Insurance Application Fee to			
807. Assumption Fee			
808.			
809.			
810.			
811.			
900. Items Required By Lender To Be Paid In Advance			
901. Interest from to @$ /day			
902. Mortgage Insurance Premium for months to			
903. Hazard Insurance Premium for years to			
904. years to			
905.			
1000. Reserves Deposited With Lender			
1001. Hazard insurance months@$ per month			
1002. Mortgage insurance months@$ per month			
1003. City property taxes months@$ per month			
1004. County property taxes months@$ per month			
1005. Annual assessments months@$ per month			
1006. months@$ per month			
1007. months@$ per month			
1008. months@$ per month			
1100. Title Charges			
1101. Settlement or closing fee to			
1102. Abstract or title search to			
1103. Title examination to			
1104. Title insurance binder to			
1105. Document preparation to			
1106. Notary fees to			
1107. Attorney's fees to			
(includes above items numbers:)			
1108. Title insurance to			
(includes above items numbers:)			
1109. Lender's coverage $			
1110. Owner's coverage $			
1111.			
1112.			
1113.			
1200. Government Recording and Transfer Charges			
1201. Recording fees: Deed $; Mortgage $; Releases $			
1202. City/county tax/stamps: Deed $; Mortgage $			
1203. State tax/stamps: Deed $; Mortgage $			
1204.			
1205.			
1300. Additional Settlement Charges			
1301. Survey to			
1302. Pest inspection to			
1303.			
1304.			
1305.			
1400. Total Settlement Charges (enter on lines 103, Section J and 502, Section K)			

FIGURE 7.3 Continued.

Source: HUDCLIPS, http://www.hudclips.org/sub_nonhud/cgi/pdfforms/1.pdf.

For example, you are considering buying a house for $90,000. Your goal is to earn a *net* profit of 20 percent within three months. It clearly would not be accurate to just multiply $90,000 by 20 percent to calculate what you need to accomplish. You need an accurate formula that takes into account both buyer's and seller's closing costs. Assuming that you calculate buyer's closing costs at 3 percent and seller's closing costs at 9 percent, how much do you need to sell this house for to net out the desired 20 percent profit? Your buyer's closing costs will be about $2,700, so the adjusted purchase price will be $92,700.

To estimate the required gross selling price you need, estimate its level using the following suggestion: increase the required markup of 20 percent by adding another 10 percent to it:

$$20\% + (20\% \times 10\%) = 22\%$$

Next add the 9% estimated closing costs plus an additional 10%:

$$9\% + (9\% \times 10\%) = 10\% \text{ (rounded up)}$$

The two estimates of 22% plus 10% come out to 32%. Increase the adjusted purchase price by 32% to estimate the required selling price:

$$\$92,700 \times 32\% = \$29,664$$

$$\$29,664 + \$92,700 = \$122,364$$

To test this, calculate it with closing costs in mind:

Estimated sales price before adjustments	$122,364
Less: 9% closing costs	<u>11,013</u>
Adjusted sales price	$111,351
Adjusted purchase price ($90,000 + 3%)	<u>−92,700</u>
Estimated profit	<u>$18,651</u>
Percentage ($18,651 ÷ $92,700)	20.1%

The worksheet in Figure 7.4 is useful for making the calculation.

Estimated Sales Price

Worksheet

Profit goal   _____ %

Profit goal × 110%   _____ %

Estimated closing costs   _____ %

Closing costs × 110%   _____ %

Total markup estimate   _____ %

Purchase price $ _____

Plus: _____ % closing costs $ _____

     Adjusted purchase price $ _____

     × markup estimate   _____ %

     Estimated sales price goal $ _____

Check:

     Sales price $ _____

     Less: _____ % closing costs $ _____

        Adjusted sales price $ _____

        Less: Adjusted purchase price $ _____

        Profit $ _____

          Percentage (profit / adjusted purchase price)   _____ %

FIGURE 7.4   Estimated Sales Price Worksheet

These calculations are not precise. The actual required sales amount will vary based on the percentages of closing costs on both sides, and also on the percentage of gain you hope to achieve. You may have to play with the numbers to back into an accurate preadjusted sales price to set your goal. The exercise is essential, however, as demonstrated above. In this case, the $90,000 purchase would need to be sold at $122,364 in order to make a net profit of 20 percent. Due to the adjustments for closing costs, the unadjusted purchase price needs to rise by nearly 36 percent, just to make that 20 percent markup work out:

$$\$90,000 \times 136\% = \$122,400$$

This is significant and worth keeping in mind. Anyone new to property flipping may use this rough guideline: As a general rule, you need to *double* your estimated profit goal in order to net out to it.

In the previous example, you bought a house for $90,000 with the intention of earning a net profit of 20 percent within three months. You cannot simply multiply $90,000 by 120 percent and assume that you need to sell for $108,000. If you did so, you would earn far less than your goal, because of your buyer's and seller's closing costs (based on the estimates in the example of 3 percent and 9 percent). Those closing costs would equal $2,700 and—based on a selling price of $108,000—$9,720, for a total of $12,420, so the actual outcome in this case would be:

Sales price	$108,000
Less: Seller's closing costs, 9%	−9,720
Adjusted sales price	$98,280
Purchase price	$90,000
Plus: Buyer's closing costs, 3%	2,700
Adjusted purchase price	$92,700
Net profit	$5,580
Net return	6.2%

The calculation of net return in this case is based on purchase price before closing costs, since the adjusted sales price was a multiple of the original $90,000. This demonstrates that merely multiplying the purchase price by the desired profit is inadequate. Applying the rule of thumb that you need to double the desired goal, an estimated requirement would employ 40 percent (twice the desired 20 percent level):

$$\$90,000 \times 140\% = \$126,000$$

In the actual example, the actual 36 percent requirement dictated the need for a sales price of $122,400, fairly close to this more realistic level.

The point to be made concerning this is that property flippers need to not only make a dramatic gain in a short period of time; they also need to allow realistically for closing costs. With this in mind, high-volume property flipping is more easily achieved profitably by working directly through a real estate broker who is willing to share equity in lieu of a commission; or obtaining a real estate sales license and acting in the role of agent and dealer. If a broker is willing to eliminate the entire 6 percent commission on a sale, it also cuts out the requirement to make such a wide margin of profit. Returning to the previous example, you would be would be able to reduce seller's closing costs from 9 percent down to 3 percent. Now the numbers look much different. Employing the same "double your required return" rule ($90,000 plus 40%):

Estimated sales price before adjustments	$126,000
Less: 3% closing costs	−3,780
Adjusted sales price	$122,220
Adjusted purchase price ($90,000 + 3%)	−92,700
Estimated profit	$29,520
Percentage ($29,520 ÷ $92,700)	31.8%

Key Point

Because closing costs apply to both sides of the transaction, you need to make a far greater profit before those costs are applied, just to end up where you want in terms of net profit.

In this case, you could easily give the broker a one-third cut of the profits and still make your 20 percent return. The broker would receive $9,840 in this case, 7.8 percent of the sales price used in the illustration. This plan is advantageous to you because it provides you far greater leeway in the transaction. If you do not attain the desired level of sales, the impact of closing costs is far less likely to ruin the plan. The broker gets a cut in exchange for sharing your risks.

Eliminating the Middle Man

You might not be able to find a broker who is willing to work with you in partnership on property flipping deals. High-volume trading gives you leverage and the ability to negotiate lower overall commissions, but only to some extent. Such arrangements on listed properties would come out of the cut earned by broker and agent. Half the overall commission goes to the selling agent, who may work for a competing firm. So your ability to make these special deals on publicly listed properties is very limited.

FSBO

acronym meaning "for sale by owner," status of properties placed on the market directly by their owners and excluding real estate agents.

Because of this limitation, you need to seek private sales. Once the property gets listed on the local MLS, any brokerage firm is free to locate a buyer and bring an offer to the table. You can work directly with a broker and, as the dealer, you bring deals in and execute them. Nevertheless, it might take a while to build up volume and to gain the credibility you need. This raises another question, however: Do you need to work with a broker? Why can't you specialize in the *FSBO* market? This "for sale by owner" approach will completely eliminate the need for commission or for giving a broker or agent a cut at all.

The main inhibiting factor to this approach is the size of the potential property flipping market. You maximize your profit by eliminating

---

Key Point

If you can arrange an equity-sharing deal with a broker, you get much greater flexibility in how much markup you need. But finding these special deals is not always possible. Brokers might be more tuned in to the more standard, uniform, less imaginative MLS listing.

Key Point
Real estate agents match buyers and sellers. But they are not valuable for completing paperwork and other requirements of the deal. For that you need an escrow agent or attorney.

the broker and salesperson, but the FSBO market is very small compared to listed properties. This should not stop you from specializing in the unlisted properties market. It simply means you need to expand your network and become an expert at finding and moving properties that are not listed publicly.

If you work directly with individuals interested in selling their homes without an agent, you have an advantage. You not only avoid real estate commissions; you also avoid the need to work with a real estate broker and share the profits. In fact, by working directly with sellers, you drastically reduce the overall cost of the transaction. While the market is more difficult to find, you can be very effective in making yourself known as a person interested in buying directly from sellers. This is a market where many discount opportunities may be found.

Many people hesitate—on both sides of the transaction—because they have come to believe that a real estate agent is essential in protecting their interests. A real estate transaction involves a lot of money, and people trust real estate agents to ensure that the proper forms are used and completed in the right manner and that nothing important is left out.

The truth is, real estate contracts are standard forms. You can complete your own contracts without any special training, and without taking any unnecessary risks. It is a simple matter of knowing what has to be covered and making sure you fill out the form correctly—which is nothing other than what real estate agents do when offers are presented.

You still need to be aware that a potential seller may be apprehensive about working with a buyer directly. The real estate industry has

Valuable Resource
You can buy standard real estate contracts online. Check www.ourfamilyplace.com/homeseller/contracts.html for real estate and other agreement forms, which are available for every state.

done a good job of convincing the public that they are essential in the transaction, and that is not the case. The agent is useful for getting exposure to the widest possible market, but the agent does not and cannot offer legal advice. (Real estate agents are not trained in the law. Though many know how to fill out these forms, they are not especially well versed in the legal matters that you need to know.)

The perfect solution to help both sides in the transaction is to open an escrow account as soon as possible. If you do a heavy volume of work in property flipping, you will be able to establish a relationship with a local escrow company who will handle the entire transaction for you. This is where the real paperwork, filing, and money exchange takes place. In fact, once a deal is signed the real estate agent normally ends his or her involvement and provides no further guidance (unless problems come up during the transaction, in which case the agent *should* be available to mediate between buyer and seller if needed).

The escrow agent provides the following services:

1. *Collecting all money required from both sides.*
2. *Paying out charges for inspectors, appraisers, and prorated expenses.*
3. *Providing all proper contracts and other forms and getting them signed and notarized.*
4. *Filing and recording all forms required locally.*
5. *Closing the deal; collecting funds from buyers and lenders and paying out those funds based on the contract.*
6. *Arranging for title search and issue of a title insurance policy.*
7. *Filing final recording documents transferring title.*

None of these services require a real estate agent. In fact, agents do not do any of these tasks, so their only value is in bringing buyers and sellers together. If you are able to find your own sellers (and later, your own buyers) you can avoid a lot of expense and make more profit on your own, whether operating as dealer or retailer.

Key Point

The escrow agent becomes your most valuable ally after the real estate agent's job is done. If you can find your own deals, you do not need a real estate salesperson at all.

Underpriced versus Totaled Property

In locating properties to flip, you will be continually looking for that essential discount. Be aware, however, that there is a vast difference between discounted properties offered for sale by motivated owners and properties needing so much work that they are totaled.

Most people who have bought and sold cars understand all too well the concept of an asset's being totaled. When a car needs more work than it is worth, there is no choice but to junk that car, take whatever money the insurance company offers, and start all over. But even though the same logic applies to real estate, it is easily forgotten.

If a property is for sale for $90,000 and you expect to net a 20 percent return, that goal works as long as you do not have to put any work into the house. Recall from the previous example that you would need to sell that $90,000 house for about 36 percent more to net out at 20 percent profit. But this is based on an important assumption—that the house does not require any repairs.

The various illustrations based on that $90,000 house showed what you would need to accomplish pricewise based on 3 percent buyer's closing costs and 9 percent seller's closing costs. A sale of about $122,400 was estimated to provide about $18,000 in net profit or about 20 percent based on purchase price of $90,000. What happens if you need to put in $20,000 in repairs just to sell the house? In order to command $122,400 on the market, the house might need those repairs. In fact, it may have been available for $90,000 specifically because it needed $20,000 in work.

In this case, the discount was not a discount at all. This house would be totaled based on your profit goal versus the repair level. So if you expect to make a net profit of $18,000 but you would also need to perform $20,000 in repairs, the transaction cannot be justified. Exceptions to this general rule include three situations:

1. *You can perform the work yourself.* You can justify buying the property if the majority of the work involves labor, *and* you have the skill to do the work yourself. In this situation, your *sweat*

Key Point

Most people know a car can be totaled. But it is not as obvious that a piece of real estate can be totaled as well. In those cases, it is not usually worth the money to try and salvage a house.

sweat equity
a property's equity that grows as the result of an owner's work to improve property value, as opposed to increases based on growing demand.

equity is quite valuable as it adds value. If you are willing to put in the time and effort to make the profit, you may be able to justify the purchase.

2. *You are willing to convert the house to a long-term hold.* You may also justify buying a house with substantial repair needs if you intend to hold for the long term. In this instance, your "flip" could take a year or longer. Ideally, rental income covers all of your expenses while you perform repair work over time. It is often the case that repairs are difficult when tenants are in the property, but it is not impossible. You may need to work out a deal with tenants allowing you to perform work while they are away.

3. *You believe market values will outpace today's estimated values.* The most speculative situation will be based on your belief that property values will grow enough to outpace the current conditions. Thus, your $18,000 profit versus $20,000 in needed repairs is based on today's values, but you believe property values will rise dramatically in the short term. If the plan involves depending on growth in market value, you take a considerable risk based on ever-higher demand. If you are right, you can make a nice profit. If you are wrong, you can lose a lot of money or be forced to convert to a long-term hold just to avoid the loss of capital.

The expectation of profit is not always what actually occurs on the market. Demand tends to change more rapidly than supply. Judging supply is relatively easy. You can analyze what is on the market and study projects under way or planned. Demand, however, is the more elusive side of valuation.

Flipping properties depends entirely on how well you can judge valuation of properties as well as the overall market. In the next chapter, an important aspect of valuation—the role of appraisers and inspectors—is studied to show how property condition affects valuation.

Key Point

Converting a flip to a long-term hold is a worthwhile strategy as long as it is preplanned and not your only way out of a bad deal.

Chapter

A Closer Look
Inspections and Appraisals

Analyzing your property flipping venture ensures that no surprises occur—at least not in your beginning assumptions. Once you know how much profit you want to achieve, you can proceed with confidence.

In locating bargains, seek the deep discount, that property whose value is set for quick sale, in need of cosmetic and low-cost repairs, or appreciating quickly in a strong current market. Furthermore, if you work only with private sellers, or make an equity deal with a broker directly, you can cut out the commission upon sale, which is usually the largest seller's closing cost.

So with preparation and planning, you can judge the market according to local conditions. Much of the preparation work requires networking, making yourself known to local lenders who may want to get defaulted properties out of their portfolios; investors for whom you want to work as a dealer or scout; real estate agents and brokers who are willing to work with you in private sales without making listings public; and, of course, sellers. You should also pay attention to two of the most important contacts you can make—and that you need—to complete both a purchase and a sale. These are the appraiser and the inspector.

> ### Key Point
>
> Property flippers are effective networkers. The more contacts you have in the real estate industry, the better you can find and complete profitable deals.

The Appraisal Process

Most people have a general idea of what appraisers do, but operate under a misconception about how real estate valuation works. The *appraisal* is a process in which an individual estimates a property's value, based on the cost of replacement or based on market value of comparable properties. This is *not* an absolute; the appraisal is only an estimate, and there is no hard-and-fast rule for determining a property's exact value. Ultimately, *market value* is the price that a buyer and seller agree upon for the sale of property.

appraisal

a process of evaluation of a property for the purpose of estimating current market value. This is based on a study of replacement cost as well as market value of comparable properties in the same area or in similar areas.

market value

the current value of property; the price at which a buyer agrees to buy and a seller agrees to sell.

The appraiser should be qualified to make the judgment about a home's value. However, this qualification varies depending on who hires the appraiser, what standards he or she sets, and the purpose of the appraisal. A local lender may have a relatively low standard for appraisal and may even send out a loan officer to make an appraisal. While the bank employee can be experienced in the sense of having completed many appraisals, the resulting opinion is not as solid as that of a trained and licensed professional appraiser. This is not a problem for the bank, whose purpose is only to establish with reasonable certainty that the property is worth enough to justify taking the risk in granting a loan.

> ### Key Point
>
> Not all appraisals are alike. Some are formal and time consuming, while others are completed informally, often by the lender directly.

Valuable Resource

Find out more about services and referrals to local appraisers at the Appraisal Institute, www.appraisalinstitute.org.

Appraisers are licensed by most states to perform appraisal for a fee. As distinguished from the informal appraisal performed by a lender, professional appraisers are hired as outside experts by real estate salespeople (to list properties), lenders (for mortgage loans), attorneys (for estates or divorce proceedings), or individuals. In addition, the primary appraisal trade association, the Appraisal Institute, provides professional training and designations for the industry.

These designations include the *MAI* (a commercial appraiser) and the *SRA* (for residential work). Because the Appraisal Institute is the result of a merger of two other organizations, these abbreviations have no specific meaning. They were originally "Member Appraisal Institute" and "Senior Residential Appraiser." This organization currently has a trademark on the designations and promotes them by letters only.

MAI
the designation of a commercial real estate appraiser awarded to qualified members by the Appraisal Institute.

The MAI must pass 11 separate examinations after 380 hours of classroom instruction. Additionally, applicants have to pass a two-day comprehensive final examination and hold a four-year degree from an accredited school. They are also required to accumulate 6,000 hours of experience, half of which must be in specialized appraisal work.

SRA
the designation of a residential real estate appraiser awarded to qualified members by the Appraisal Institute.

The SRA is required to pass six exams after 200 hours of classroom work, and must hold an associate's degree from an accredited school. The SRA must also demonstrate at least 3,000 hours experience over at least a two-year period.

Key Point

A professional designation is not a requirement for appraisers. A state license is required, however, and rules vary by state. So it is essential to check out qualifications before picking an appraiser.

The professional designations are not absolute requirements to work in the field. The state licenses are far more important and are required for anyone performing appraisal work for a fee. Most lenders perform less detailed appraisal work on their own, which saves time and money, and real estate agents will provide opinions to homeowners about home values. But the most important qualification for those charging a fee is that they have a state license. Qualifications vary, but most states require some type of testing and qualification before people are allowed to establish estimates of property values.

In comparison to an appraiser, local county and city governments hire an *assessor* to set values of properties. The assessor usually has some background and experience as an appraiser, although this is not always a requirement. The assessor sets values for determining the level of property tax obligations locally. The individual may be an employee or may run for the office publicly, in which case the "qualification" for the job may be more political than experience-based. In that case, the appraiser works as an administrator and probably supervises other employees, who go out and look at properties to set assessed value. Because the assessor works for the city or county, the assessed value of properties may not directly indicate true or full market value.

assessor
a city or county employee responsible for setting property values for the purpose of setting property tax liabilities.

Appraisal Methods for Residential Property

The appraiser may use several methods or a combination of methods to estimate values. It is important to also remember that appraised value is likely to vary based on the purpose of the appraisal. For example, a bank may do a cursory appraisal to ensure that the property is where the borrower said, in fairly good shape, and comparable to other properties in the neighborhood. In such an appraisal, valuation will be based not only on the drive-by appraisal but also on the public record in the assessor's office and in the recorder's office. The assessor's record provides assessed value and indicates whether property taxes are current or past due. The recorder's office verifies the name of the current owner.

In comparison, a real estate agent may order an appraisal on behalf of a seller, in which case the agent probably is hoping for a high-end estimate. An attorney, however, can also order an appraisal as part of setting

> ## Key Point
>
> The purpose of the appraisal will affect the conclusion. The appraiser is aware of who is paying the bill, and valuation can be determined within a broad range of possibilities.

a stepped-up basis in an estate in order to aim for a low-end appraisal. If an attorney calls for an appraisal, the desired result depends on who has hired the attorney. If the spouse is trying to establish value for his or her share of the estate, then the higher the better; but if the spouse is trying to arrive at a settlement he or she will be required to pay, a lower estimate would be preferred.

These variations in the property value do not imply that appraisal is dishonest or inaccurate. But the appraisal itself is nothing more than an opinion. As long as the appraiser is able to justify the outcome on some fair basis, there will be a wide range of possible valuations. It depends on which comparable properties are used and how the appraiser decides to make the comparison, either favorably or unfavorably. The comparable properties represent sales in the recent past (usually one year or less), so in a region with a healthy volume of transactions, the appraiser has latitude to pick and choose the comparables used in the appraisal. It is a science with a lot of room for interpretation.

Several appraisal methods may be used. The *income approach* is used for properties that produce income, usually multiunit residential (apartments, for example) or commercial properties. Under this approach, the appraiser studies income productivity of comparable properties and arrives at a *gross rent multiplier (GRM)* for comparable income properties, which can then be used to set value of the *subject property*.

For example, if recent sales of comparable income properties averaged $390,000 and monthly

income approach

an appraisal method used for valuation of investment properties and based on income potential of comparable properties in the same area. The income approach is based on development of a gross rent multiplier (GRM), which is then applied against the subject property to estimate market value.

gross rent multiplier (GRM)

a calculation used by appraisers as part of the income approach. The sales prices of other income properties are divided by income to arrive at GRM; then the average GRM factor is multiplied by rents in the subject property to arrive at value.

subject property
the property being appraised.

rent averages were $3,000, the GRM would be 130.0—the GRM factor. If the subject property's monthly rents are $3,180, the income method appraisal is:

$$130.0 \times \$3,180 = \$413,400$$

The income method is more complex; this illustration is provided only to make a distinction between income property appraisal and methods used for single-family residential property. Even if you flip single-family homes, they will be appraised using the standard residential methods described in the next paragraph. The income approach is appropriate only for multiunit residential and for commercial properties.

cost method
an appraisal method used to estimate what it would cost to duplicate a house as it stands today.

replacement cost
an appraisal estimate of the cost to replace a home as it exists today, given the possibility of exceptional architecture or handcrafting.

Residential appraisal takes one of two forms, and a standard approach is to summarize both methods in the appraisal report. The appraiser may give more weight to one method or the other. The first is the *cost method*, an estimate of what it would cost to replace the house in its existing condition. A distinction has to be made between the cost of a relatively modern building and *replacement cost* of an older one. Replacement cost for older homes with exceptional architecture or handiwork could be far more expensive than the relative cost of replacing a home of the same size and the same number of rooms.

The cost method is a popular appraisal method because it enables the appraiser to use local costs per square foot of materials, which is very reliable in the appraisal estimate. However, the cost value will be reduced due to *depreciation* on

Key Point

Replacement cost is not always identical to current building costs. If a property has exceptional craftsmanship or architecture, replacement cost may be much higher than the well-known cost per square foot of construction.

the property. This is not the same application as that used for tax purposes, in which a capital asset is written off and the cost recovered over a period of years. In appraisal, depreciation refers to a reduction in the cost basis due to condition and *economic life* of the property. So a run-down or obsolete property is depreciated to a greater extent than one that is in great shape with remodeled kitchen, baths, and modern systems in place.

depreciation
a reduction in the current cost or replacement value of property to reflect true value based on condition.

Appraisers estimate economic life by dividing a base of 100 by what is assumed to be the economic life of the property. For example, if the appraiser believes that the house has an economic life of 45 years, then annual depreciation is:

economic life
an estimate of a property's potential life based on quality of construction, depreciation, and any upgraded or renovated areas.

$$100 \div 45 = 2.22\% \text{ depreciation per year}$$

The appraiser would next estimate the *effective age* of the property, which is not the same as the age based on the year built; effective age is an appraiser's estimate of the property's age based on current condition. If the house is 10 years old but the appraiser believes that its effective age is 12 years, then the annual depreciation would be applied against the effective age rather than the years since it was built:

effective age
the age of a property based not on actual years since it was built, but on current condition; used to calculate annual depreciation from cost or replacement value.

$$2.22 \times 12 = 26.64\% \text{ depreciation}$$

The cost method is only the first of two methods appraisers use for appraising residential property. The second is called the *market or sales comparison approach*. This is a direct analysis of the subject property with

---

Key Point

The "effective age" of a property is not necessarily its actual age. Effective age is determined by a property's condition. So a run-down property will appraise for less than one that is well cared for.

Key Point

Appraisal is very subjective. Valuation of property depends on which comps are picked, and on how the appraiser judges the value of adjustments. That leaves a lot of "wiggle room" in the outcome.

---

market or sales comparison approach

an appraisal method used for residential properties, involving a study between the subject property and other properties that sold recently in the same or similar neighborhoods, and sharing the same or similar characteristics.

recent sales of properties sharing the same characteristics: overall size, style, number of rooms, and neighborhood. Ideally, the comparison should be made to recent sales in the same neighborhood or in neighborhoods that tend to be valued at the same level. A sale one month prior would clearly be more comparable than one 11 months prior; and a home a block away would be a more desirable comparable property than one across town.

The appraiser finds 'comps' and writes them up in the appraisal report. Two or three properties are usually compared in this manner. Adjustments are then made for any differences between comps and the subject property: age, condition, number and size of rooms, lot size, and anything else the appraiser believes affects value. Thus, the adjustments can be either additions or subtractions from value.

The selection of comps and the nature and degree of adjustments is highly subjective. In this process the appraiser relies on professional experience and judgment, but a lot of latitude is given to this expert opinion and there is no absolute point of agreement among appraisers how to arrive at a true value for a specific property.

Working with the Appraiser

In the final analysis, an appraisal—which is nothing more than a professional opinion—is likely to conform to an overall estimate of property values within the city or town, and more specifically given the type of property, lot size, neighborhood, and other factors. If appraisals are exceptionally high or low compared to other appraised values, then the appraiser making poor judgments would not be able to continue in this work. The client (lender, real estate salesperson, investor) would discover that poor judgment would have disastrous consequences on the market—for buyers as well as for sellers.

The best-known sequence of events is that a potential buyer goes to an open house or walks into a real estate office. Eventually, buyers find a home they like and put an offer on the home. An appraisal may already exist or, if not, a lender will order one. The buyer will pay for the appraisal as part of the loan processing and this ends up as one of the buyer's closing costs.

This is not the only way to proceed. As a property flipper, you do not have to accept the usual course of events at all. This applies whether you work directly with sellers or make arrangements to work with a lender. For example:

1. *When you buy, get an appraisal directly and pick your appraiser.* As one of the early steps in the negotiation process, get your own appraisal. If the seller already has an appraisal, that does not mean it is useful to you. Remembering that a potential valuation range is possible, the seller's report may be higher than a buyer's appraisal report. Also pick the appraiser yourself. Do not depend on a real estate salesperson or lender. The appraiser should know he or she is working for *you.*

2. *When you sell, pick your own appraiser and get the appraisal early.* If you get your appraisal on your own, pick the appraiser and get a report before speaking with buyers. By controlling which appraiser you use, you are able to ensure that the appraiser understands what you want. If you are sending a lot of business to one appraiser, you are more likely to get fast turnaround on written reports as well.

3. *When working as a dealer, make sure you know the source of an appraisal.* If your property flipping involves you as matchmaker between buyer and seller, you need to ensure that there will be enough markup for you to profit. This means you need to

---

Key Point

You save a lot of time and money getting your own appraisal. This also allows you to control the process and speed up the transaction.

control as much of the deal as possible, including the appraisal. For example, if you are exercising an option to sell a property, you will have no money in the deal other than what you have paid in lease payments and option premium; but a buyer may require an appraisal report (if not directly, the buyer's lender will certainly want one). By getting an appraisal first, you have control and a tremendous advantage. When buyers find out that a seller has already gotten an appraisal, it is rare for them to object. Few people understand that an appraisal is subjective, so the assumption is that the appraisal is fair and accurate. The more common reaction is to be glad that the seller saved them the time and expense of getting an appraisal to qualify for a loan.

The purpose of the report should be kept in mind. As a property flipper, time is usually short and you need to get through closing as rapidly as possible. If you intend to turn over properties quickly, it is best to have both seller and buyer in a single closing even though this is not always possible. Since you will likely go through two closings, one as buyer and one as seller, you want to cut as many time elements out as possible.

Remember, the longer it takes to close, the higher your costs will be. This is especially true if you need to carry a loan for a period of weeks (or months). So you need to identify the points in which the process is most likely to be held up. These are:

1. *Appraisal delay time.* When real estate volume is high—best condition for property flipping—a limited number of qualified appraisers are overworked. This leads to delays that can run into weeks of added days in escrow. Even if appraisals have been completed, it takes time to prepare reports, involving photographs of comps, analysis, calculation, and actually drafting the document. You get around this problem by having your appraisal completed before selling the property.

Key Point

The greatest efficiency in reducing closing costs is to use as many of the same reports as possible on both sides. As long as a short period of time has passed, you can cut out a lot of the usual time-consuming and expensive steps.

---

2. *Lender review of buyer's application.* As a buyer, you want to have a deal worked out with a lender. You can be prequalified, for example, which is a smart step for property flipping. You also should look for a local lender with the authority to speed applications through the process, and who is flexible enough to work with you in an accelerated schedule. You can also refer potential buyers to "your guy," who can process the loan more rapidly than the impersonal, larger institutional lenders.

3. *Satisfying inspection and repair work contingencies.* Deals without contingencies may be desirable in terms of speed. But they are not always possible. As buyer, you want to ensure that no undisclosed work is required, so you may want the contingency in your contract. If you flip the property quickly, it is to your advantage to have a recent written inspection report. You can offer a copy to your prospective buyer, saving money and time in the process. Additionally, remember that contingency work can proceed while lenders are reviewing applications and other closing matters are moving forward. Find an escrow company willing to fast-track the process by executing different tasks at the same time.

4. *Contingencies for financing approval or sale of other properties.* The most troubling types of contingencies involve working with buyers who have not been preapproved or whose offer is contingent on selling another property. These contingencies can and do hold up sales indefinitely; and a large number of offers end up failing because would-be buyers are not qualified by a lender or are unable to sell their current homes by the contractual deadline. In fact, some buyers put these contingencies into offers as a type of escape clause for the deal. As a property flipper, you should emphasize that buyers need to get qualified by lenders before making offers. You may also decide to reject any offer including a contingency to sell another home. It just holds up the process too long and does not allow you any control over the timing of the deal.

Key Point

Property flippers may decide to reject any offers including contingencies for the sale of another home. That can ruin the whole concept of fast turnover.

> **Key Point**
>
> The title search does not have to wait until the last minute. It can be done the day after you sign the contract, and then updated with a last-minute final review.

5. *Title search.* The title search is a process of examining the public record to ensure that no liens, mortgages, or judgments have been filed against the property. A mortgage, tax lien, delinquent tax, or court judgment means that the liability goes with the property. A title insurance company keeps a "bank" of records that duplicate recordings in one area of all liens on property. By checking their bank, the title insurance company can determine whether any unknown liens exist. Once the title search is completed, the company issues a title insurance policy, which protects you in case the title search did not find a lien and it comes up later. With title insurance, you would not have to pay the debt; the title insurance company would be responsible. That search takes time. Some escrow agents will tell you that the search cannot be done until just before closing in case a lien were filed in the weeks before—this is not true. The title search should be ordered immediately after the contract is signed. Then, right before closing, the title search is updated for the days since the initial search, which is a simple process. This two-part evaluation of recorded liens happens regularly.

If you can fast-track all of the functions that normally hold up closing—and refuse to accept contingencies out of your control—you can execute a closing of property very quickly. Working with the right lender, escrow company, appraisers, and inspectors, a closing that would normally take 45 to 60 days can be cut back to 21 to 30 days.

Inspections: Eliminating Contingencies

Besides finding and working with appraisers who give you fast turnaround, you also need to locate inspectors who understand the special time constraints of property flipping. There are three general categories of inspectors:

1. *Pest inspectors.* The "termite inspection" is well known in the southern states and over time most homes get some degree of infestation. Even outside of the termite-prone states, other pests can cause damage as well, including beetles and ants in dozens of varieties. A pest inspection should be executed, even if it is not required by state law. As the buyer, you should plan to ask for a pest inspection early on and include the contingency in your offer. As seller, make sure you control who performs the inspection. If you plan to do a lot of property flipping, a pest inspector is an essential member of your team.

2. *Specialized inspection consultants or companies.* Some properties require specialized types of inspections. So if the property has structural problems or defects, or the topography is problematic, a soil engineer or structural expert may be required. Environmental hazards can also pose complex problems and understanding the scope and expense of those problems may also need additional inspection work.

3. *Home inspectors.* A qualified, professional home inspector examines the entire property. A written report should always be provided, along with a guarantee or warranty that no undisclosed problems exist within the scope of what the inspector looked at. The inspector should not be a contractor who will also offer to fix problems, and a professional inspector should not refer you to anyone else. The inspector should be entirely independent. Locate a local member of the American Society of Home Inspectors (ASHI) for this work. (Check www.ashi.org to find qualified local people.)

Inspection work is normally required via contingencies, and just as you save time and expense by hiring your own appraiser, you can cut time and expense from the property flipping transaction by hiring an

---

Key Point

Everyone has heard of the termite inspector who carries around his own small jar of termites to plant on the scene. Infestation, however, is common enough that this does not happen often. Even so, find one inspector you trust and send all of your business to that inspector.

Key Point
One good solution to the problem of delay through contingencies is to combine your purchase and sale into a single closing. This is not easy to accomplish—but it will save a lot of time and cost.

inspector early. If you flip within a short period of time, a single inspection can serve your needs as buyer and seller.

You need to be able to demonstrate to your buyer that an inspection was performed within the past few months and that any defects found in the report were fixed. So, as you make repairs indicated in the inspection report, keep all of the documents. As seller, you remove the need for contingencies on the part of the buyer by delivering all of the documentation needed:

- Appraisal report
- Qualified inspection report
- Documentation of repairs and improvements
- Pest control reports

The more work you do early on in the property flipping process, the more time and expense you save on the other end. All of the steps you execute as buyer produce documents, and these can be used when you sell as well. As long as the documentation is fairly recent—less than one year old, for example—they can be used. And if you can prove that you fixed all of the problems uncovered during home and pest inspections, you are saving the buyer money and time while removing contingencies from the deal.

What remains, however, is potentially the greatest delay of all: financing. This problem exists for you as buyer as well as when you sell. The next chapter explores the overall problems of financing, notably for nonowner-occupied investment properties, and offers solutions.

Chapter

Find the Money
Financing Plans for Flips

The best-laid plans ultimately succeed if you can get your hands on the money. Structuring a deal with no cash is difficult, especially when you're just starting out. You are going to need a source for financing in the majority of situations.

The exception to this is one in which you provide an owner with a lease option, rent the property to someone else and create positive cash flow, and exercise the option *at the same time you sell the property*. In this situation, you make a profit in the markup and you have no cash into the deal. These kinds of transactions can be clean and efficient, but they are not always easy to find or to put together.

If you will need to take an equity position—or even to be prepared to do so even if you end up flipping before you close—you are going to need to demonstrate to a seller that you are able to finance the purchase.

Key Point

Your property flipping program might look good on paper, but you have to be sure you can finance the plan, or it simply will not work.

Finding the Right Commercial Lender

The difficulty in going to the most obvious place—the commercial lender—is that most institutions are inflexible, not to mention unimaginative. All of their loans conform to the same standard, and lenders are accustomed to working with people who are buying a home (rather than an investment) and whose income is easily verified. So if you are self-employed or want to invest in property rather than live in it, you start out being a huge problem to the commercial lender. This is so for many reasons.

secondary market

a market consisting of quasi-governmental agencies that collect home mortgages; bundle them with other, similar mortgages; and sell shares to investors.

mortgage pool

an investment program structured like a mutual fund but consisting of secured home mortgages rather than stocks or bonds.

In addition to wanting all loans to look the same and be easy to process, commercial lenders usually conform to the rules of the *secondary market.* In the structure of home mortgage lending today, very few lenders carry loans in their portfolio. They process loans and verify income and credit, but as soon as the loan closes, it is often transferred to a *mortgage pool,* where it is bundled with other, similar home mortgages.

The organizations managing large numbers of home loans through this secondary market include the FNMA (Federal National Mortgage Association), also called "Fannie Mae"; the GNMA (Government National Mortgage Association), also called "Ginnie Mae"; and the Federal Home Loan Mortgage Corporation, also called "Freddie Mac." These organizations take over mortgages from commercial lenders and sell shares, so that no individual bank or savings institution needs to commit funds to long-term mortgages.

The flow of funds loaned out through commercial institutions is shown in Figure 9.1.

Valuable Resource

To learn more about secondary market investments, check three websites: www.fanniemae.com, www.ginniemae.gov, and www.freddiemac.com.

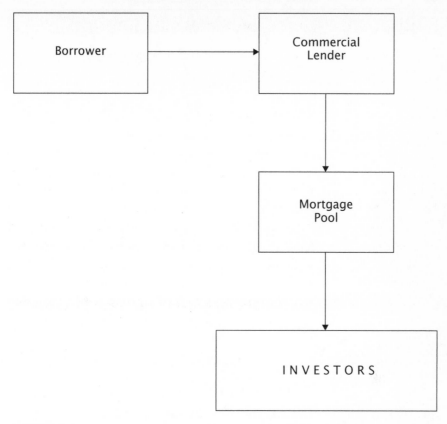

FIGURE 9.1 Flow of Funds through a Commercial Institution

The advantage in moving mortgages from banks and other institutions to mortgage pools is that it makes more money available. Individual investors, buying incremental shares in the mortgage pool, finance the growth in mortgage lending while earning interest on a bundle of *secured debts*—a desirable advantage over many other forms of debt investing.

The institution continues to *service* the loan so that the change is invisible to the borrower. So the borrower makes payments to the bank, which in turn forwards the payment to the mortgage pool.

secured debts
all debts involving a form of collateral, such as mortgage loans, which are secured by the value of property. In comparison, risks are much higher for unsecured debts such as promissory notes or corporate debentures; in the event of default, unsecured debts are more difficult to collect.

Key Point

Banks and savings institutions rarely carry their own loans; these are more often sold on the secondary market.

service

in lending institutions, the collection, processing, and recordkeeping of mortgage loans, even after the loan has been assigned or sold to another lender or to a mortgage pool.

Because secondary market rules are very specific, lenders cannot be creative in the ways they structure loans. For example, borrowers have to meet criteria for income and cash flow, and these criteria have to be met unless the lender is willing to carry the loan as a *portfolio loan*, meaning the bank lends out the money directly and carries the loan on its books, rather than assigning it elsewhere. It is very difficult to find a lender willing to write loans directly. So, if you are looking for a creative solution with a lender, commercial institutions are not likely sources for property flipping financing.

portfolio loan

a loan carried by a lender on its own books and with its own money loaned out, and not assigned to another lender or to a mortgage pool.

The Burden of Nonowner-Occupied Properties

You face an additional obstacle even if you do borrow money from a commercial lender. While a homeowner can qualify for a loan under fairly liberal terms, investors are held to a higher standard.

A homeowner can get a loan at prevailing mortgage rates and for little (sometimes nothing) down. This is the case because owner-occupied property tends to be the safest type of mortgage. With relatively low rates of foreclosure, the secondary market rules for owner-occupied loans are easily met.

Key Point

Because lenders have to conform to the restrictions imposed by the secondary market, investors—even property flippers—often do not qualify for loans that they would qualify for if the property were to be owner occupied.

Key Point

As an investor, you are going to have more difficulty finding loans for rental property than for your own home. This means you will have to pay bigger down payments and higher interest rates.

Investors are normally required to pay a higher rate of interest and, often, one or more points as a cost of getting a loan. You might also be required to make a down payment considerably higher than a homeowner would need to make. Some institutions require investors to put as much as 30 percent down. For this reason, many real estate investors have found that it is easier to convert their current homes to rental investments, and apply for loans on new properties as primary residences. This is a game played between investors and lenders. The investor applies for a loan for a new *primary residence* and, soon after closing, decides to convert the new property to a rental or flip instead. Lenders will tell you that as long as you "intend" to live in the property through the closing of escrow, you are free to change your mind the following day.

primary residence
for tax purposes, a person's residence for calculation of tax-free sales. A primary residence must be occupied for at least 24 months out of the past 60 months.

This is an uncomfortable reality; but the rules of the secondary market have made it common. Conceivably, you could buy one property after another under the owner-occupied standards as long as you state your intention to occupy the property and then convert it immediately after escrow closes. The practice is questionable at best and is not advisable. Some investors may find alternatives.

Valuable Resource

You are allowed to exclude up to $500,000 (for a married couple) or $250,000 (if you are single) on the sale of your primary residence. You must have occupied the property for at least two of the past five years, and the only limit on how often you can sell tax-free involves time. You can execute a tax-free sale of your primary residence only once per 24-month period. Check www.irs.gov/newsroom/article/0,,id=105042,00.html to review the rules and restrictions for the exclusion.

Key Point

Some real estate investors have figured out ways to work around lender restrictions. If you are willing to change your primary residence every two years, you can avoid taxes on your profits and qualify for owner-occupied financing.

If your current residence has appreciated in value, you may buy a new property that would be a viable flip candidate (in terms of its current price at a discount from market value) and sell your residence. By moving into the newly acquired property, you conform to the lender rules. By selling your appreciated property at a profit, you can make the transaction tax free.

If you look at this series of transactions and the potential advantages they offer, the concept solves two problems. First, it enables you to qualify for the new loan. Second, you take your profit on your current home tax free. This "reverse flip" strategy makes sense if:

1. *You and your family are willing to move.* An investment program might seem good on paper, but if it causes disruption or unhappiness for your family, it probably is not worth the trouble. A young couple with no children and an entrepreneurial spirit are best suited for frequent moves; but if you are settled and you have children in school, a move—even within the same city or town—can be terribly disruptive.

2. *The transaction in your current home will be profitable.* The reverse flip idea is sensible if you have a net profit in your current home. You take that profit tax free, making it possible to *lower* your mortgage payments as part of the exchange.

3. *The new property is available at a discount and suitable for your family.* The same rules should apply for any flip: You need to get the property at a discount from current market value. If this is not possible, you need to believe that market values are rising quickly enough to justify moving. This may be the case if your current home is in a neighborhood that is not appreciating, and you plan to move to a home in a neighborhood where values are on the rise.

The reverse flip—selling your current home and changing primary residences—makes sense under these qualifications. It also gets around the restrictions placed on investors in terms of interest rates and down payment.

Interest-Only and Bridge Loans

Most property flippers are concerned with having to make loan payments, even for a short period of time. The longer you have to hold on to a flip property, the lower your profit will be, so the need for financing presents a serious problem.

Two potential solutions are found in alternative lending formats. First is the *interest-only loan*, which is a loan for which you make no principal payments. You pay only interest each month, which reduces your payments. For example, a 30-year fully amortized loan for $100,000 at 7 percent costs $665.31 per month. The same loan on an interest-only basis requires monthly payments of $583.33.

interest-only loan

a mortgage loan requiring interest payments only and no reduction in principal. An interest-only loan usually also requires payment at a specified due date in the future.

Useful Tip

To compute monthly interest (on interest-only loans or on fully amortized loans), follow these steps:

1. Multiply the loan balance by the interest rate:

$$\$100,000 \times .07 = \$7,000.00$$

2. Divide this annual interest by 12 (months):

$$\$7,000.00 \div 12 = \$583.33$$

3. In the case of a fully amortized loan, subtract the interest from the full payment to find the principal:

$$\$665.31 - \$583.33 = \$81.98$$

4. Finally, subtract the principal from the beginning loan balance to find the new loan balance forward:

$$\$100,000.00 - \$81.98 - \$99,918.02$$

Key Point

An interest-only loan may appear the best alternative for property flipping. However, if you end up keeping the property longer than you originally intended, interest expense can easily absorb your profit.

---

bridge loan

a type of loan intended to serve as a short-term replacement for longer-term and more permanent financing, or to carry the mortgage debt for a short period of ownership in property.

balloon mortgage

a mortgage in which interest-only payments are made for a term of months or years, and the entire principal balance is due in full at the end of the term.

The interest-only loan may also be called a *bridge loan,* although bridge loans are not always interest-only. A bridge loan is intended to carry you through a relatively short holding period and is a perfect solution for property flipping. The loan may even include a provision requiring no payments whatsoever for a period of time, such as three months. Lenders expect to be paid with interest when you sell the property. Another variety is called the *balloon mortgage,* in which interest-only payments are made and the entire amount of the loan is due at a future date. The bridge loan is a smart alternative for property flipping if you are certain that you will sell the property before the repayment date arrives.

The interest-only (or bridge) loan and the balloon mortgage are excellent devices for property flippers as long as they are short term in nature. Some borrowers proceed on the premise that growth in real estate market values will outpace the cost of borrowing, so they are not concerned with how long it takes to sell the property. This is a mistake.

Remember that the longer it takes to sell property, the more you pay in interest. Also remember that the higher your interest rate and dollar obligation, the less likely you will make your property flipping goal. Some borrowers even seek out loans below the required repayment level to aid cash flow. Many lenders provide these types of loans because they are profitable, but they are expensive for investors. When the monthly payment is lower than the monthly interest obligation, the loan is set up for *negative amortization,* meaning the debt rises each month instead of falling.

> ### Key Point
>
> Negative amortization is doubly expensive for property flippers. First, you suffer ongoing interest payments. Second, even as you pay interest, your mortgage balance rises each month.

For example, a lender may offer a loan at a current 1 percent rate, but with an annual interest obligation of 7 percent. This loan will increase in balance each month. Your payment is based on 1 percent interest-only payments, but monthly interest is far higher. The first three months' payments of a $100,000 loan would look like the summary in Table 9.1.

negative amortization condition in a loan when monthly payments are lower than the monthly interest owed. As a consequence, the loan balance rises each month.

In the case of negative amortization, compound interest works against you. Your loan balance rises each month because the payment is not high enough to cover interest. It *might* work out that real estate values exceed this shortfall, but that is an added risk that changes the entire structure of the investment.

Negative amortization loans are offered to homeowners as an incentive to refinance. So when you hear an ad on TV or receive a notice in the mail advising that you can refinance a $250,000 loan for payments of $312.50 per month, you should be able to quickly tell that you will have negative amortization. A 6 percent loan will cost $1,250 in interest each month:

$$(\$250{,}000 \times .06) \div 12 = \$1{,}250$$

TABLE 9.1   Negative Amortization Loan Payments

Month	Obligation 7%, 30 years	Interest Payment @ 1%	Obligation Less Payment	Loan Balance
Balance				$100,000.00
January	$665.31	$83.33	$581.98	100,581.98
February	665.31	83.82	581.49	101,163.47
March	665.31	84.30	581.01	101,744.48

So you can figure out right away that a $300 payment will not come close to covering interest at 6 percent. In fact, this monthly payment would calculate at 1.5 percent per month. The way to calculate this is to perform the interest calculation in reverse:

$$(\$312.50 \times 12) \div \$250,000 = 1.5 \text{ percent}$$

annual percentage rate (APR)

the actual interest a borrower is obligated to repay annually on a mortgage loan.

If you read the fine print in these offers, you discover that the loan includes an *annual percentage rate (APR)*, which is the actual rate you are obligated to pay.

So when you see the ad, it will promise that your $250,000 loan can be refinanced for monthly payments of $312.50. But if you read the fine print you will discover that the APR is 6.00 percent. This means that your loan balance will be *rising* every month. In this example, the difference between interest alone ($1,250) and the monthly payment ($312.50) is $937.50 for the first month. This additional loan obligation will rise each month, because the shortfall adds to the outstanding balance.

fixed-rate mortgages

financing for real estate based on an interest rate that does not change over the entire term. For example, a 30-year fixed-rate mortgage maintains the same interest rate throughout the term.

Traditional Mortgages

In evaluating your financing choices beyond interest-only and other creative solutions, you will invariably also want to consider traditional *fixed-rate mortgages* and *variable-rate mortgages*. Either of these may serve as worthwhile alternatives to other loans, all depending on the actual length of time you intend to keep properties.

Whichever type of mortgage you select, an excellent credit rating is essential to making your

---

Key Point

Some wording in loan ads is deceiving. Do not be fooled by the promise of unrealistically low monthly payments. This usually involves negative amortization and, overall, a very expensive mortgage.

> ### Key Point
>
> Every real estate investor needs an excellent credit history. This opens up many doors and financing alternatives. But without excellent credit, you are prevented from pursuing the best property flipping opportunities.

property flipping plan work. With an exceptionally good credit history, you can obtain financing with little problem, even for investment property. If your credit is poor, you will have to shop around for financing and, in all probability, you will have to pay a premium in interest rates based on your credit history.

variable-rate mortgages
also called adjustable-rate mortgages (ARMs), these loans contain provisions for periodic changes in the interest rate based on one of several loan rate indexes.

The fixed-rate mortgage is most appropriate if you plan to keep a property for several months or for many years. You pay higher interest to lock in the fixed rate, so the longer you plan to keep the property, the greater the safety in the fixed rate mortgage. This is especially true if interest rates have been volatile and you consider it likely that rates will rise over the course of time that you own the property.

A variable-rate mortgage may be available with significantly lower rates. The risk in these loans is that interest rates may increase in the future, so that your loan's rate will increase as well. But if you plan to dispose of the property within one year or less, this will not matter. Once you sell the property, future increases in interest will not be of concern. So for short-term turnover of investment properties, you should pick the variable-rate loan.

A review of the usual variable-rate terms may help you in deciding between one type of loan and another. The variable-rate mortgage is

> ### Key Point
>
> The variable-rate mortgage is usually the most practical choice for property flipping. You benefit from short-term low interest rates since you do not plan to keep the property long enough for higher rates to kick in.

"tied" to a predetermined interest rate index. In other words, future increases or decreases in your loan's rate will be based on the degree of change in the index. Typical indexes include those based on interest rates for U.S. government securities, such as the Treasury one-year constant maturity (12 MTA) rate and one-year, two-year, or three-year series maturities for Treasury securities. Some lenders use regional rates in place of national ones, and it is worth comparing how various indexes have performed in recent months in comparison to overall interest rate trends.

teaser rate

an exceptionally low initial interest rate offered with a variable-rate mortgage, which is replaced in 6 to 12 months by a higher market rate.

The variable-rate mortgage includes a number of provisions that will further help you to decide which deal is the best. Be aware that some loans are marketed with an exceptionally low initial interest rate, called the *teaser rate*, which lasts only six months to one year. After that time, the rate jumps to a higher rate closer to market rates.

The teaser rate is actually an advantage to you if, in fact, you intend to sell the property within the period the teaser rate will be in effect. For example, if typical rates for investment properties are 7.5 percent today and you can get a one-year rate of 4.0 percent, you should definitely pick that loan—as long as you plan to sell in one year or less.

payment cap

a provision in a variable-rate mortgage limiting the maximum payment a borrower is required to make.

Every variable loan also has a series of "caps" or maximums. A *payment cap* limits how much your total payment can rise during the life of the loan. At first glance, the payment cap looks reassuring. When you consider the outcome, however, it could be an expensive provision. If interest rates exceed your payment level, you end up with negative amortization. Therefore, even as you make your maximum contractual payment, your loan balance would rise each month.

A more practical type of cap actually contains two separate provisions. The *rate cap* places a limit on how much the lender can increase

---

Key Point

A low teaser rate is a lender's trick. But property flippers can turn this into an advantage. If you plan to sell the property before the teaser rate expires, you will reduce your overall interest rate.

your interest rate. The provision defines the period involved in such increases (usually 6 months or 12 months); it also defines the maximum increase than can be applied at each review. A *lifetime cap* limits the overall maximum interest a lender can charge over the entire mortgage period. For example, a loan may specify that the starting rate is 6.5 percent; that the interest rate can be changed as often as once per year; that the maximum increase per year is limited to 1.5 percent; and that the lifetime cap is 6.0 percent, so the maximum interest rate can never be higher than 12.5 percent.

The variable-rate loan interest rate can drop as well as rise. If the index on which the loan is based falls, so will the interest rate. Lenders often add a *floor rate* specifying the minimum rate that has to be paid on the loan, so even if the index rate would take the variable-rate interest below that floor, the rate is frozen there. So with the floor rate and the lifetime cap, both lenders and borrowers are able to define the overall range of interest on a loan over its entire life.

Using Your Home Equity

If you approach property flipping purely as an investment plan, separate from your family home, you would never consider placing your home at risk to finance the property flipping plan. That is prudent for many people. Keeping your residence safe and sound and allowing your equity to grow over time makes sense most of the time.

rate cap
a clause in a variable-rate loan defining the maximum interest rate increase a lender can place on a loan, including the frequency that changes can occur.

lifetime cap
a clause in a variable-rate loan defining the maximum interest rate increase a lender can add to the beginning balance over the entire period of the loan.

floor rate
the minimum interest rate that is charged on a variable-rate loan, even if the underlying index would take the rate below the floor level.

Key Point

The combination of a lifetime cap and a floor rate enable variable-rate mortgage borrowers to know, even far into the future, the full range of possible interest rate they will have to pay.

Depending on your point of view about your home equity, however, you might be willing to use the equity in your home to increase the
range of property flipping opportunities. This is appropriate in the following circumstances:

1. *You are willing to take the risk.* More than any other criterion, you
   need to be able to understand and accept the risks in using your
   home equity for investment purposes. Borrowing money on your
   home increases your monthly payment and places greater strain
   on your monthly budget. So you need to be sure that you appreciate the potential hazards involved.

2. *Your home equity has grown substantially.* The plan to use home
   equity also makes sense if and when your equity is substantial.
   That is money available to you, and for some people untouched
   equity is idle money. This is not completely true, because equity
   is also a form of financial security; but as long as you understand
   the risks and you want to access the equity, it can be used to
   finance property flipping.

3. *You believe that property flipping conditions are excellent.* Property
   flipping makes sense only in conditions where property values
   are growing rapidly. In such conditions, using equity could be
   highly profitable. You should also remember that these conditions can change suddenly. As one of the risks of borrowing on
   your home equity, you need to be aware of what will occur if you
   end up not being able to sell a property for a profit. What happens if you have to sell at a loss or convert the property to a long-
   term rental? These risks may change your perceptions of home
   equity and how you may put it to work.

4. *You have a short-term exit strategy.* The use of home equity is
   most appropriate when you plan to go in and out of ownership
   in a relatively short period of time. If you have a plan to exit
   within three months or less, that would usually be the most

appropriate range in which to employ home equity for financing property flipping programs.

The most obvious way to access your home equity is through *refinancing* of your current mortgage. This is a good way to remove cash, but it also reduces your home equity and increases your debt. So you need to ensure that money removed through refinancing will more than offset this added debt burden.

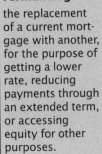

refinancing
the replacement of a current mortgage with another, for the purpose of getting a lower rate, reducing payments through an extended term, or accessing equity for other purposes.

The refinancing of your mortgage is permanent; your investment, however, is temporary. So this may become a serious point worthy of evaluation if you decide to refinance. This is not to say refinancing is necessarily a poor idea. Indeed, there are situations in which refinancing makes sense for property flipping.

If you can take money out and, at the same time, reduce your payment, then you may justify the long-term added interest. When you take out cash and reduce your monthly payment, that is the result of two possible causes or a combination of both. First is the extended loan term (for example, your current mortgage would be paid off in 15 years, and you replace that with a 30-year mortgage), which means you will pay much more interest over time. This also extends the cash flow requirements on your personal budget.

The second reason that payments are reduced is when you are able to replace the current mortgage with one containing a lower interest rate. This is justified as long as you plan to remain in your current home long enough to recover your closing costs through reduced payments. This *breakeven term* may be anywhere from a few months to several years.

breakeven term
the number of months required in a replacement mortgage to offset the closing costs incurred.

Key Point

Refinancing to flip properties is often overly expensive. In addition, the higher mortgage burden is permanent, whereas the property flip is short term.

> ### Key Point
>
> Evaluate the feasibility of refinancing by figuring out how long it will take to recoup your closing costs. Do you plan to keep your home at least that long?

For example, if your closing costs are $4,150 and your monthly payment is reduced by $148, then your breakeven term will be approximately 28 months. This is computed by dividing the closing costs by your monthly savings:

$$\$4,150 \div \$148 = 28 \text{ months}$$

With this term in mind, the question is whether you are planning to remain in your home for more than 28 months. If you were planning to sell in one year, refinancing would not make sense. The closing costs exceed the breakeven term.

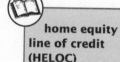

home equity line of credit (HELOC)

a secured line of credit based on your home equity; the borrower pays interest only when funds are drawn, and is allowed to repay borrowed amounts as quickly as possible without penalty.

An alternative to refinancing is the *home equity line of credit (HELOC)*. This is a line of credit tied to your home equity; thus, it is a secured line of credit. It is economical because most lenders allow you to have a HELOC with very little in the way of closing costs. A $50 annual fee is typical, and lenders may approve your HELOC application if you provide a current assessor's statement on your home.

The HELOC is available to you, but you only pay interest on the amount you actually draw out, and then only until it is repaid. There is no penalty for rapid repayment of HELOC funds. These devices are cheap and convenient. Many lenders provide HELOC customers with a checkbook to use for accessing their funds.

For property flipping, the HELOC may be the perfect type of loan, for a number of reasons. As with all forms of borrowing money to invest, you need to understand the risks involved and be willing to access your home equity and, possibly, to end up with more debt than you intended. The HELOC provides several advantages:

> ### Key Point
>
> The HELOC is the perfect device for property flipping (assuming you are willing to use your home equity). It is affordable, flexible, and convenient.

1. *Interest is deductible as an itemized deduction.* Real estate investors are allowed to deduct the expenses related to their activities. Anyone who holds rental property and claims deductions is limited to a maximum of $25,000 per year in losses (less if your adjusted gross income is higher than $100,000). So anyone with a lot of property and reported losses may have to carry those losses over to future years. When you access your home equity to finance your property flipping purchases, interest is deducted on federal Schedule A as itemized deductions. So even if you reach your maximum allowance, you can still deduct interest each year.

2. *You can borrow money short term and repay quickly without penalty.* The HELOC is economical. Unlike the traditional mortgage loan, you can move in and out of the debt position. So if you complete a property flipping transaction in five weeks, you can use HELOC funds and then repay the entire amount as soon as your transaction closes. There is no penalty for repaying the debt.

3. *You pay interest only for the time money is outstanding.* Your total interest expense is limited only to the time the money is outstanding. In a traditional mortgage, interest is assessed each month, whether you are putting borrowed funds to work or not. And the only way to reduce that interest is to pay off the loan. In a HELOC arrangement, you have control over how much you borrow, and this can vary from one transaction to the next.

4. *There are no recurring closing costs to access your funds.* With a traditional mortgage, you have to pay closing costs each time you borrow money. This includes appraisals, title search and insurance, and lender's points. These costs can add up to thousands of dollars. With a HELOC, you can borrow and repay money as often as you wish, and there are no costs other than the annual fee the lender assesses and the interest on outstanding balances. This

---

Key Point

The many benefits to the HELOC make this a compelling alternative to refinancing. As long as you are willing to access your home equity for property flipping, the HELOC solves many of your financing problems.

---

makes the HELOC the perfect tool for financing your property flipping program.

5. *You only have to qualify once.* Lender policies for investments are more restrictive than those for homeowners. This means higher interest rates and more down payments, not to mention needing to qualify on the basis of income. But with a HELOC tied to your home equity, you do not have to go through a lender's qualification for every transaction. HELOC approval does not restrict how you use the funds. This saves you a lot of time and expense, not to mention avoiding the possibility of a lender's rejecting your mortgage application.

Private Lenders

Yet another alternative is to find a private lender to finance your property flipping program. This can be a real estate broker or an entrepreneur interested in making a profit on secured mortgages.

The problem with private lenders is the same problem with refinancing through a conventional lender—inflexibility. A private lender usually wants to lend you all of the funds you need and receive interest on a regular basis. Due to the nature of property flipping, this can be an expensive process.

bankable
reference to a property's qualification for financing based on a lender's requirements, usually due to structural minimum rules.

In some cases, you can convince sellers to carry loans for you. This works for many property flippers, but not for all. Many sellers want to get their cash out of the deal and be able to walk away. If a seller offers to carry a loan for you, caution is advised. This may be part of the deal because the house is not *bankable*. This means the owner cannot get a conventional loan, due to some structural problem or other cause. A lender may require a house to have a foundation; so a house built with post-and-beam supports would not be bankable.

> ### Key Point
>
> Be cautious when sellers are willing to carry financing on their homes. You need to make sure you know why. Remember, a seller's problems become *your* problems when you get ready to sell.

So if and when a property is not bankable, the seller knows that you, as a potential buyer, are not going to be able to finance the purchase through the normal channels. In fact, were you to try to get a conventional loan, the property's structural limitations would be likely to kill the deal. The seller, then, is left with no choice but to offer to carry a loan for you, just to make the deal happen.

Because you are interested in flipping the property, you need to stay away from any properties that are not bankable. Remember, when you as a buyer take on a seller's problems, those become *your* problems when you become the seller.

Any arrangement including seller financing may be proposed by you. When the seller offers it, however, you need to take a careful look at the property before agreeing to those terms. It could turn out to be impossible to flip the property unless you agree to carry a loan for a new buyer; and that is contrary to what most people want to do when they enter a property flipping strategy.

The next chapter extends the financial discussion to explain the federal tax rules governing real estate investing and property flipping.

10

Uncle Sam Steps In
Tax Rules for Flipping

A s soon as you become involved with real estate—in any aspect—you soon discover that the tax rules in this field are complicated. This should not discourage you. As a real estate investor, you have many advantages not available to most investors.

Real estate is usually classified as a passive activity under Internal Revenue Service rules. A "passive" investment is one in which the investor is not involved in day-to-day management. Passive losses can only be applied against passive gains from other activities and, if not used in one year, have to be carried over and applied to a future year.

Real estate investing is the one exception to this rule. Although it is passive, you are allowed to deduct losses up to a specific limit, which is explained in this chapter. Losses are likely to occur because you can deduct depreciation on real estate. Depreciation is a calculated expense and not an actual out-of-pocket expenditure. So it is entirely possible for real estate investors to achieve positive cash flow *and* still report a net loss. This is where the great advantage is derived for real estate investors.

For most property flipping activities, in which you plan to hold property for as short a time as possible, the depreciation rules do not apply. But realistically, many property flippers end up holding some real estate for longer than just a few weeks; so the passive loss and depreciation rules—and limitations on deductions—do apply.

Key Point

Although passive losses cannot generally be claimed on your federal tax return, real estate is the only exception. This makes real estate investing exceptional, due to this one feature.

activity
under the federal tax rules, the nature of investment that determines how much you may deduct in losses. This determination is based on time you spend on investments and the degree of control you have over decisions.

participation rules
the activity investors exhibit in buying, holding, and selling real estate and in the amount of time spent, degree of control, and decision-making power.

To complicate matters further, you might also be exempt from the passive loss deduction rules if you qualify as a real estate professional.

Activity Rules for Real Estate

When you invest in real estate, your *activity* determines your status and whether you are allowed to deduct losses. For tax purposes, your activity is going to qualify you as either an investor or as a real estate professional, and the difference is important.

There are two kinds of activity distinctions—these are called *participation rules* because they are based on how you conduct your real estate investments. You might be able to deduct only a specific amount of passive losses based on participation; or in some instances, property flippers can deduct all losses regardless of the amount.

Two kinds of participation are used to decide how much you can deduct in real estate losses. First is *material participation*, which applies to a substantial business operation. Second is *active participation*, which applies to most real estate investors, including property flippers.

Key Point

To qualify under the rules of active participation, you have to directly manage your properties and make decisions regarding purchase, sales, and payment of bills.

The material participation rules that might apply to property flipping—if you do this full time—are explained later in this chapter. To qualify as an active participant (and thus be allowed to claim deductions for net losses) you are required at a minimum to make decisions concerning each property that you own. If you flip properties without renting them out, the decision concerning when to sell and for how much qualifies for this distinction. If you hold properties, you need to be involved in setting rental rates, screening and approving tenants, and paying expenses. So if you delegate all of the responsibility to a management company, you would not be allowed to deduct losses.

The tax rules require that you analyze cash flow on an after-tax basis. Otherwise, you cannot accurately estimate cash flow. Tax benefits are such a significant factor in the calculation of cash flow that it cannot be ignored. So you need to exercise *tax planning* as part of your real estate program.

Tax planning is not a casual activity. It should be part of a recurring process. You may need to meet with your tax advisor two or more times per year. The proper time for tax planning is in advance. In order to minimize tax liabilities in any year, you may need to plan your transactions ahead of time. If you own a property that you can sell at a profit, should you sell by the end of the year? Or should you wait until after December 31? The decision should be based on your overall income and tax liability, and how a sale in the current year would affect your status.

The process of timing transactions to minimize taxes, or to increase taxable income in the current year, is called *tax avoidance*. This is perfectly legal. As long as you follow the tax rules, you

material participation

the status of a full-time real estate professional who, if qualified, is allowed to deduct all real estate losses without limitation.

active participation

status of a real estate investor. If the individual makes management decisions concerning properties, he or she is allowed to deduct up to $25,000 in annual losses from real estate investing.

tax planning

the forward-looking estimate of tax liabilities and, for real estate investors, tax benefits arising from real estate activities, coordinating real estate timing and decision making with the rest of a person's portfolio and as part of overall income and tax status.

tax avoidance

the preplanning and timing of transactions to reduce tax liabilities or to maximize current-year loss deductions by matching them against gains.

can decide to sell property sooner than originally planned or defer a sale to reduce taxes. There are situations in which increasing this year's capital gains would make sense. If you suffered a large capital loss this year in your stock portfolio, you may want to sell real estate in the same year. The maximum deductible capital loss is $3,000 per year. So if you can match gains against current-year losses, you can exclude taxes from selling your real estate.

Maximum Deductions per Year

The tax rules specify that the maximum loss you can deduct per year from real estate investments is $25,000. This applies to you as a real estate investor, but if you are a real estate professional, you are not restricted to this limitation. As a property flipper, you are likely to be classified as an investor and subject to the annual limits.

capital expenditure

amounts spent to improve or maintain property, which have value beyond the current year. These expenditures are treated as long-term assets and have to be depreciated over many years.

The $25,000 maximum includes rental income minus expenses, including depreciation. Deductible expenses include interest, property taxes, utilities, maintenance, and all other expenses related directly to managing your property. Any *capital expenditure*, such as a new roof or adding a fourth bedroom, cannot be deducted but has to be set up as an asset and depreciated.

The $25,000 maximum deduction is subject to some qualifications. Generally speaking, you can claim the full $25,000 if your *adjusted gross income (AGI)* is under $100,000. Above $100,000, the allowable deduction is reduced by 50 cents for each

Key Point
For many people, the loss limitation is a problem due to high adjusted gross income. If you qualify under the rules as a real estate professional, you can deduct all losses regardless of amount.

additional dollar. For example, if your adjusted gross income was $110,000, your maximum allowable deduction goes down by one-half the excess, or $5,000; so you would be allowed only $20,000. After $150,000 of adjusted gross income, the deduction disappears and is not allowed.

The actual adjusted gross income reported on your tax return is not the number you use to determine your qualification. The calculation has to be based on what is called the *modified adjusted gross income*. This number becomes important when your income is close to or above $100,000. It is your reported AGI, adjusted to add back reductions for individual retirement account (IRA) contributions, student loan interest, taxable Social Security benefits, self-employment tax, and tuition.

The modified AGI can make a difference in what you are allowed to deduct. There are cases where your AGI appears to qualify you for the full $25,000 deduction; but using the modified AGI, the deduction is limited. For example, if your AGI was $97,000 and the sum of disallowed items was $11,000, your loss deduction would be less than $25,000:

adjusted gross income (AGI)
for federal tax purposes, total taxable income reduced by specific adjustments but before calculating exemptions, itemized or standard deductions.

modified adjusted gross income
reported adjusted gross income without certain deductions, such as IRA contributions, student loan interest, Social Security benefits, self-employment tax, and tuition. Adding these items back to AGI increases the modified AGI and may reduce allowable real estate loss deductions.

Adjusted gross income	$97,000
Plus: disallowed deduction	−11,000
Modified AGI	$108,000
Maximum income level	−100,000
Excess	8,000
One-half of excess	4,000
Maximum deduction allowed	$25,000
Less: One-half excess income	−4,000
Loss limitation	$21,000

In this example, an individual with $95,000 AGI loses $4,000 of deductible losses due to the modifications required under the law. As

> **Key Point**
>
> Modified adjusted gross income has to be used to calculate maximum deductibility of losses. Essentially, this removes most of the adjustments to gross income claimed on your federal tax return.

long as net losses for the year are $21,000 or less in this situation, the full amount can be deducted. But any excess above $21,000 has to be carried forward and used in future years.

If your adjusted gross income is close to $100,000 or above that level, you may need to calculate cash flow and net profit or loss in a different manner than for anyone whose income is under those levels. If your modified AGI is at or above $150,000, no deduction from real estate investing is allowed (except for real estate professionals). Because so many investors are able to benefit primarily because of the tax benefits in deducting losses, this is an important distinction.

Real Estate Professionals and Taxes

Some property flipping activity falls into a different category than the passive activity limitations most investors have to live with. If you flip properties as your primary business activity, you might be allowed to deduct losses even if they are higher than $25,000.

A real estate professional is someone who meets specific criteria:

1. You must spend more than half your time in a real property business (such as flipping properties or working as a dealer or scout).

2. You must spend 750 hours or more per year in the business.

If you meet both of these tests for each type of activity (for example, if you combine property flipping and management of rental properties), you could be called a real estate professional. But even a real estate professional has to "materially" participate in order to be allowed to deduct losses above $25,000 per year (or to escape the upward income reductions).

Generally speaking, you need to be able to establish that you are involved in real estate on a "regular, continuous, and substantial" basis to qualify for the material participation test. To ensure that you meet these rules, consult with your tax advisor. The IRS publishes guidelines for the number of hours required and the time period you need before you can qualify for material participation.

If you do qualify, you are not subject to the $25,000 annual limitations, and the total of your adjusted gross income does not matter. Your property flipping and other real estate activity that qualifies under this rule is considered as business income rather than as investment activity. This may have ramifications for how sales of property are treated. While investors enjoy a lowered tax rate for long-term capital gains (on properties owned one year or more), there may be circumstances in which real estate professionals are not allowed to claim the lower rate. Income may be treated entirely as *ordinary income*, which is taxed at your effective tax rate and not subject to any special reductions.

ordinary income

an individual's taxable income, subject to published rates and not qualified for lower rates applicable to long-term capital gains, or excluded from tax due to investment rules.

The basic rules for deducting real estate expenses apply to investors and to real estate professionals, and they are subject to the same definitions. The treatment of net income and calculation of taxes, however, differs considerably.

Allowed expenses you can deduct include property taxes, insurance, interest on mortgage loans, utilities, and depreciation. You can also deduct the cost of any other expense that you can prove is directly related to your real estate activity (whether as a business or investment). This includes advertising, auto and truck expenses, office supplies, telephone, and professional fees.

For any expense deductions you claim, you should have some form of proof. This includes invoices, statements, receipts and other paper. Paid checks are also valid forms of proof, and if your activity volume is significant, you should also set up a separate bank account and move all transactions through that account. Separating your investment and

Key Point

Deduction of business or investment expenses applies to all individuals, whether classified as investors or real estate professionals. The only difference between the two is the ceiling on loss deductions.

business activities from your personal financial records is required. It is also a wise idea. It is far easier to keep track of your profit and loss and cash flow when you keep separate books than if you mingle transactions in with your family's income and expenses.

Because real estate accounting and taxation is so complex, you probably also need to hire a qualified tax professional. This does not mean merely going to a tax preparation company and giving them your receipts. Your consultant should be able to also advise you on the tax rules, tax planning and methods of legal tax avoidance, and analysis of proposed transactions with tax benefits and consequences in mind.

Depreciation Basics

Among the various tax rules, depreciation is one of the most complex. But it is not difficult to get a basic idea of how it works.

useful life
an estimate of an asset's reasonable utility, and the basis for calculating depreciation.

Depreciation is simply the writing off of the cost of real estate over a period of years. Unlike current-year expenses, which are deducted each year, capital assets like real estate have to be depreciated over time. The period of time over which assets are depreciated is called the asset's *useful life*. This is an estimate, in general terms, of the number of years an asset will last, and the depreciation rules divide assets into specific classes for that purpose.

book value
the net value of an asset, representing its purchase value minus depreciation.

The useful life is somewhat misleading, because it implies that at the end of that term the asset will be worthless. In practice, some assets—notably real estate—tend to increase in market value, even as the *book value* declines due to depreciation. One

---

Key Point

Real estate is depreciated until improvements fall to zero—so "book value" of property may be quite low. At the same time, actual market value of real estate is likely to rise, often substantially, above book value.

flaw in modern accounting practices is that assets always reflect ever-falling book values even if their true market value is rising.

In the case of real estate, land can never be depreciated but is always shown on the books at purchase value. For corporations that own land, the current value is always the purchase price and improvements on that land, including the buildings, that are depreciated over many years until the book value of improvements falls to zero—even if market value is many multiples above original purchase price.

Today, most assets—including investment real estate—are depreciated under a system called the *Modified Accelerated Cost Recovery System (MACRS)*. This system has been developed over many years and as a result of reforms in the rules modifying the original Accelerated Cost Recovery System (ACRS). Under MACRS, some assets—especially computers, autos and trucks, and office equipment—can be depreciated using *accelerated depreciation*, a system in which more expense is claimed in the early years and less later on.

Real estate cannot be depreciated under the accelerated method. Both residential and commercial real estate has to be depreciated using the *straight-line depreciation* method. Under MACRS, residential real estate has to be depreciated over 27.5 years and commercial real estate over 39 years. In both cases, land cannot be depreciated.

Every asset is classified into an appropriate *recovery period*, which defines the number of years and depreciation method to be used. In those recovery periods involving accelerated depreciation, you can elect to use the straight-line method. If that election is made, however, it has to be applied to all assets in that recovery period acquired in the same year.

Modified Accelerated Cost Recovery System (MACRS)
the most commonly used system for calculating depreciation on investment and business assets, which includes defined periods over which depreciation applies and the depreciation methods to be used for each type of asset.

accelerated depreciation
a calculation allowed for some assets, in which more depreciation is claimed in earlier years and less in later years.

straight-line depreciation
a method of calculating depreciation in which the same amount is claimed each year until the asset has been fully depreciated.

recovery period
one of several asset classifications used for calculating depreciation. For non–real estate depreciated over either five or seven years, accelerated depreciation is allowed. For real estate, only straight-line depreciation is permitted.

In addition to the 27.5-year residential and 39-year commercial real estate recovery periods, two additional, shorter recovery periods are applicable to real estate investors. So-called five-year property includes autos and light trucks, office machinery and computers, landscaping equipment, and appliances. Seven-year property includes office furniture.

Calculating Depreciation

Depreciation is reported on IRS form 4562, which is shown in Figure 10.1.

To calculate depreciation, most people refer to the published charts put out by the Internal Revenue Service and available online in the free publication, *Instructions for Form 4562*. This publication includes tables indicating percentages to be used each year for all classes of depreciation.

The five-year and seven-year classes of assets normally use the 200% method of accelerated depreciation. Under this calculation, the earlier years allow 200% of a calculated straight-line depreciation rate. Each year's new calculation is based on the asset's cost, minus the previous year's depreciation. An alternative, the 150% method, involves one and one-half times the annual straight-line depreciation, reduced each year and reverting to straight-line in the later years. Table 10.1 provides the annual percentages that can be claimed for both recovery periods under these methods.

Form **4562** (Rev. January 2006) Department of the Treasury Internal Revenue Service	**Depreciation and Amortization** (Including Information on Listed Property) ► See separate instructions. ► Attach to your tax return.	OMB No. 1545-0172 **2005** Attachment Sequence No. **67**
Name(s) shown on return	Business or activity to which this form relates	Identifying number

Part I Election To Expense Certain Property Under Section 179
Note: If you have any listed property, complete Part V before you complete Part I.

1	Maximum amount. See the instructions for a higher limit for certain businesses	1	$105,000
2	Total cost of section 179 property placed in service (see instructions)	2	
3	Threshold cost of section 179 property before reduction in limitation	3	$420,000
4	Reduction in limitation. Subtract line 3 from line 2. If zero or less, enter -0-	4	
5	Dollar limitation for tax year. Subtract line 4 from line 1. If zero or less, enter -0-. If married filing separately, see instructions	5	

(a) Description of property	(b) Cost (business use only)	(c) Elected cost
6		

7	Listed property. Enter the amount from line 29	7		
8	Total elected cost of section 179 property. Add amounts in column (c), lines 6 and 7		8	
9	Tentative deduction. Enter the **smaller** of line 5 or line 8		9	
10	Carryover of disallowed deduction from line 13 of your 2004 Form 4562		10	
11	Business income limitation. Enter the smaller of business income (not less than zero) or line 5 (see instructions)		11	
12	Section 179 expense deduction. Add lines 9 and 10, but do not enter more than line 11		12	
13	Carryover of disallowed deduction to 2006. Add lines 9 and 10, less line 12 ►	13		

Note: Do not use Part II or Part III below for listed property. Instead, use Part V.

Part II Special Depreciation Allowance and Other Depreciation (Do not include listed property.) (See instructions.)

14	Special allowance for certain aircraft, certain property with a long production period, and qualified NYL or GO Zone property (other than listed property) placed in service during the tax year (see instructions)	14	
15	Property subject to section 168(f)(1) election	15	
16	Other depreciation (including ACRS)	16	

Part III MACRS Depreciation (Do not include listed property.) (See instructions.)

Section A

17	MACRS deductions for assets placed in service in tax years beginning before 2005	17	
18	If you are electing to group any assets placed in service during the tax year into one or more general asset accounts, check here ► ☐		

Section B—Assets Placed in Service During 2005 Tax Year Using the General Depreciation System

(a) Classification of property	(b) Month and year placed in service	(c) Basis for depreciation (business/investment use only—see instructions)	(d) Recovery period	(e) Convention	(f) Method	(g) Depreciation deduction
19a 3-year property						
b 5-year property						
c 7-year property						
d 10-year property						
e 15-year property						
f 20-year property						
g 25-year property			25 yrs.		S/L	
h Residential rental property			27.5 yrs.	MM	S/L	
			27.5 yrs.	MM	S/L	
i Nonresidential real property			39 yrs.	MM	S/L	
				MM	S/L	

Section C—Assets Placed in Service During 2005 Tax Year Using the Alternative Depreciation System

20a Class life					S/L	
b 12-year			12 yrs.		S/L	
c 40-year			40 yrs.	MM	S/L	

Part IV Summary (see instructions)

21	Listed property. Enter amount from line 28	21	
22	**Total.** Add amounts from line 12, lines 14 through 17, lines 19 and 20 in column (g), and line 21. Enter here and on the appropriate lines of your return. Partnerships and S corporations—see instr.	22	
23	For assets shown above and placed in service during the current year, enter the portion of the basis attributable to section 263A costs	23	

For Paperwork Reduction Act Notice, see separate instructions.   Cat. No. 12906N   Form **4562** (2005) (Rev. 1-2006)

FIGURE 10.1 Form 4582: Depreciation and Amortization

Form 4562 (2005) (Rev. 1-2006)   Page **2**

Part V	**Listed Property** (Include automobiles, certain other vehicles, cellular telephones, certain computers, and property used for entertainment, recreation, or amusement.)

Note: *For any vehicle for which you are using the standard mileage rate or deducting lease expense, complete only 24a, 24b, columns (a) through (c) of Section A, all of Section B, and Section C if applicable.*

Section A—Depreciation and Other Information (Caution: *See the instructions for limits for passenger automobiles.)*

24a Do you have evidence to support the business/investment use claimed? ☐ Yes ☐ No   24b If "Yes," is the evidence written? ☐ Yes ☐ No

(a) Type of property (list vehicles first)	(b) Date placed in service	(c) Business/ investment use percentage	(d) Cost or other basis	(e) Basis for depreciation (business/investment use only)	(f) Recovery period	(g) Method/ Convention	(h) Depreciation deduction	(i) Elected section 179 cost
25 Special allowance for certain aircraft, certain property with a long production period, and qualified NYL or GO Zone property placed in service during the tax year and used more than 50% in a qualified business use (see instructions)					25			
26 Property used more than 50% in a qualified business use:								
		%						
		%						
		%						
27 Property used 50% or less in a qualified business use:								
		%				S/L –		
		%				S/L –		
		%				S/L –		

28 Add amounts in column (h), lines 25 through 27. Enter here and on line 21, page 1 . . | 28 | |
29 Add amounts in column (i), line 26. Enter here and on line 7, page 1 . . . . | | 29 |

Section B—Information on Use of Vehicles

Complete this section for vehicles used by a sole proprietor, partner, or other "more than 5% owner," or related person.
If you provided vehicles to your employees, first answer the questions in Section C to see if you meet an exception to completing this section for those vehicles.

	(a) Vehicle 1		(b) Vehicle 2		(c) Vehicle 3		(d) Vehicle 4		(e) Vehicle 5		(f) Vehicle 6	
30 Total business/investment miles driven during the year (**do not** include commuting miles)												
31 Total commuting miles driven during the year												
32 Total other personal (noncommuting) miles driven												
33 Total miles driven during the year. Add lines 30 through 32												
34 Was the vehicle available for personal use during off-duty hours?	Yes	No	Yes	No	Yes	No	Yes	No	Yes	No	Yes	No
35 Was the vehicle used primarily by a more than 5% owner or related person?												
36 Is another vehicle available for personal use?												

Section C—Questions for Employers Who Provide Vehicles for Use by Their Employees

Answer these questions to determine if you meet an exception to completing Section B for vehicles used by employees who **are not** more than 5% owners or related persons (see instructions).

		Yes	No
37	Do you maintain a written policy statement that prohibits all personal use of vehicles, including commuting, by your employees?		
38	Do you maintain a written policy statement that prohibits personal use of vehicles, except commuting, by your employees? See the instructions for vehicles used by corporate officers, directors, or 1% or more owners		
39	Do you treat all use of vehicles by employees as personal use?		
40	Do you provide more than five vehicles to your employees, obtain information from your employees about the use of the vehicles, and retain the information received?		
41	Do you meet the requirements concerning qualified automobile demonstration use? (See instructions.)		

Note: *If your answer to 37, 38, 39, 40, or 41 is "Yes," do not complete Section B for the covered vehicles.*

Part VI	**Amortization**

(a) Description of costs	(b) Date amortization begins	(c) Amortizable amount	(d) Code section	(e) Amortization period or percentage	(f) Amortization for this year
42 Amortization of costs that begins during your 2005 tax year (see instructions):					

43 Amortization of costs that began before your 2005 tax year . . . . | 43 | |
44 **Total.** Add amounts in column (f). See the instructions for where to report . . . . | 44 | |

Form **4562** (2005) (Rev. 1-2006)

FIGURE 10.1 Continued.

Valuable Resource

To download free forms and publications, check www.irs.gov and use the search feature to find the forms you need.

TABLE 10.1 Half-Year Convention Example, $4,000 Asset

200% Accelerated Depreciation:

5-Year Recovery Period			7-Year Recovery Period		
Year	Percentage	Amount	Year	Percentage	Amount
1	20.00%	$800.00	1	14.29%	$571.60
2	32.00%	1,280.00	2	24.49%	979.60
3	19.20%	768.00	3	17.49%	699.60
4	11.52%	460.80	4	12.49%	499.60
5	11.52%	460.80	5	8.93%	357.20
6	5.76%	230.40	6	8.92%	356.80
			7	8.93%	357.20
			8	4.46%	178.40
Total	100.00%	$4,000.00	Total	100.00%	$4,000.00

150% Accelerated Depreciation:

5-Year Recovery Period			7-Year Recovery Period		
Year	Percentage	Amount	Year	Percentage	Amount
1	15.00%	$600.00	1	10.71%	428.40
2	25.50%	1,020.00	2	19.13%	765.20
3	17.85%	714.00	3	15.03%	601.20
4	16.66%	666.40	4	12.25%	490.00
5	16.66%	666.40	5	12.25%	490.00
6	8.33%	333.20	6	12.25%	490.00
			7	12.25%	490.00
			8	6.13%	245.20
Total	100.00%	$4,000.00	Total	100.00%	$4,000.00

The decision to use one method or the other depends on whether you believe you need more deductions now or later. A comparison between these methods shows the differences in the calculations. If you are flipping properties this year but you know you will exceed the $25,000 maximum loss allowance, it would make sense to defer as much depreciation as possible. You cannot use deductions this year because your losses are above the maximum.

Key Point

Deciding to claim extended depreciation for assets is a matter of tax planning. Once the decision is made, it cannot be reversed.

midmonth convention

a depreciation rule determining first-year depreciation for real estate. It is based on dividing the year into 24 half-months and calculating depreciation on the assumption that the purchase occurred halfway through the month of actual purchase.

In deciding how to depreciate assets, two additional calculations have to be made. The *midmonth convention* is a method for figuring out the first-year depreciation on real estate. This convention assumes that all real estate purchased in any specific month was purchased exactly one-half of the way through that month. So the first year's depreciation is calculated based on a portion of the total year. If you think of a year as containing 24 half-months, the midmonth convention makes sense. So if you were to acquire real estate in March, for example, you would be entitled to 19/24ths of the year's straight-line depreciation. This excludes the five half-months for January, February, and the first half of March. This method applies only to real estate.

The applicable percentages allowed for residential real estate under the midmonth convention are summarized in Table 10.2.

TABLE 10.2   Midmonth Convention for Real Estate

Month Asset Was Placed in Service	Allowed Depreciation
1	95.83%
2	87.50%
3	79.17%
4	70.83%
5	62.50%
6	54.17%
7	45.83%
8	37.50%
9	29.17%
10	20.83%
11	12.50%
12	4.17%

The table summarizes how depreciation works over 27.5 years. In the first year, you are allowed to determine the percentage in column one based on the month you acquired the asset and placed it in service. For example, if you purchased property in March last year and the value of the improvements (total minus land) was $128,000, first calculate the annual depreciation:

$$\$128,000 \div 27.5 = \$4,655$$

Next apply the percentage in the third month from the Table 10.2:

$$\$4,655 \times 79.17\% \times \$3,685$$

This percentage is derived from the calculation of the number of half-month periods in the year:

$$19 \div 24 = 79.17\%$$

A second convention applies to non–real estate assets. This is called the *half-year convention* and it is based on a broad assumption that assets in non–real estate recovery periods were purchased halfway through the year. Any asset purchased during the year is one-half eligible for the annual calculated depreciation. Referring back to Table 10.1, you see that for five-year property, the first year's depreciation using the 200% method is 20.00 percent. A $4,000 asset under this method would normally be depreciated at the rate of 40.00 percent for the first year:

$$(\$4,000 \div 5) \times 200\% \times \$1,600$$

However, applying the half-year convention, only one-half of the indicated first-year depreciation is allowed:

$$\$4,000 \times 20.00\% = \$800.00$$

Key Point

The "conventions" for first-year depreciation are simply a way to make calculations uniform.

---

elections

decisions allowed under the rules to claim depreciation at a slower rate than provided under the rules, or to pick different depreciation methods. Most elections are irrevocable once made.

When you calculate the actual depreciation methods, you are entitled to make some *elections*. These are choices you make under the rules. Most elections are permanent and cannot be reversed once made. You can elect to claim depreciation over a period longer than the methods listed by the IRS for each recovery period. You can also extend residential real estate depreciation for longer than the prescribed 27.5 years; and you can elect to use straight-line depreciation for other assets in place of the allowed accelerated methods. The rule of thumb to remember is that you are allowed to elect to claim *less* than you are allowed in depreciation, but never *more*. Elections usually are applied to all assets acquired each year in each recovery class.

Two specific elections usually apply for property flipping or real estate investing. First is the election to use 150% accelerated depreciation rather than the more common 200%. You make this election by writing "150" on the form in the "method" column on Form 4562. The second election is one to use straight-line depreciation instead of an accelerated method. This election is applied to *all* assets for a recovery period placed into service in the year the election is made. To make this so-called "IRC Section 168 election" (reference to the Internal Revenue Code section), you need to attach a statement to your tax return, reading:

> I elect under Section 168(b)(5) to have provisions of Section 168(b)(3)(D) apply to all property placed in service in the tax year ended December 31, 20___, that was included as part of the _____-year recovery period.

The blanks are filled in with the applicable year and recovery period (for example, five-year or seven-year).

One problem arising for real estate depreciation is the question of how to calculate the base for improvements. Usually, the purchase contract includes the total purchase price but does not break that down between land and improvements. But you need to be able to make this distinction to calculate depreciation. Land cannot be depreciated, so this is an important calculation.

Key Point

Elections enable you to affect each year's level of deductions to some degree. The decision to permanently change how depreciation is claimed will not necessarily have a major impact on tax liabilities. Even so, you should consult with your tax advisor before making any permanent tax election.

You can pick one of three methods to determine the value of depreciable improvements and nondepreciable land. Whichever one you pick, it is probably wise to use that same method for all property acquired each year. This is not a requirement, but a recommendation. The decision as to which method you use should be determined by which produces the higher value on the depreciable side. If you want to claim as much depreciation as possible, select the method that results in higher improvement values. If you do not need or want the depreciation expense, go the opposite way. The key here is that the method you use to calculate values has to be documented and reasonable. The breakdown will vary by property. For example, if you buy a house on a typical building lot, it is likely that improvement value will be higher than a different property on five acres.

The three methods are:

1. *Appraised value.* The most popular method is the value set during the actual property appraisal. This is the most recent valuation; it is based on market comparisons and expert opinion; and it is usually fairly reliable.

2. *Assessed value.* The local assessor's opinion may be outdated, but can still be used. Often, when you purchase property, it is immediately reassessed and the assessed value increased to approximate current market value. One flaw in using this method is that the assessed value found in the property listing could be out of date; and you might not be able to obtain a new assessed value by the time you prepare your tax return.

3. *Insurance value.* Your insurance company will set a value on your property. They do not insure land, but the value provided in your insurance policy can be used to calculate the depreciable base of improvements.

If you employ either appraised or assessed value, the indicated value will not necessarily be equal to your purchase price. Ideally, if you want to flip properties, you will be able to purchase them below the estimated market value. To calculate how much you can set as the value of improvements, use appraised or assessed value to determine the percentage. Let us say your appraised value was $129,000, consisting of $95,000 for improvements and $34,000 for land. But you end up purchasing the property for $105,000. To calculate how much to set as a depreciable base of improvements, first calculate the percentage based on appraised value:

$$\$95,000 \div \$129,000 = 73.6\%$$

Next apply the percentage to your purchase price:

$$\$105,000 \times 73.6\% = \$77,280$$

Using this method, you would assign the $105,000 purchase price (rounded to the closest $100) as:

Improvements	$77,300
Land	<u>27,700</u>
Total	<u>$105,000</u>

Tax-Deferred Exchanges

tax deferral
a procedure allowing the delay of payment of tax this year, by carrying profits forward and applying them against replacement investment properties.

As an investor in real estate, you may qualify to avoid paying taxes until a later year. Using *tax deferral,* you can carry a profit forward to be applied to a property you buy in replacement for an investment property you sell. This is called a *like-kind exchange.* This is also called a 1031 exchange, so named for the IRC code section where the like-kind exchange rules were written.

> **Key Point**
>
> In addition to the obvious benefits of deducting annual losses from real estate activity, you can defer taxes once you sell. This makes real estate especially attractive to anyone in the upper tax rate brackets.

To accomplish a like-kind exchange, you have to meet five criteria:

like-kind exchange
a trade of one investment property for another, allowing investors to pay taxes on profits in the future rather than in the year of sale.

1. Both investments—the one sold and the replacement property—must both be real estate. But you can exchange different types of real estate and still qualify.

2. The transaction has to be completed within 180 days from the date the sale closes on the sold property.

3. The purchase price of the replacement property has to be higher than the sale price of the original property in order for the entire profit to be deferrable.

4. The exchange of funds cannot be made directly, but has to be managed through a third-party facilitator.

5. The seller of the replacement property must agree in writing to cooperate with the buyer in completing the like-kind exchange.

The way tax deferral works is that any gain is deducted from the basis of the replacement property. If you purchase a property for an

> **Valuable Resource**
>
> Check www.irs.gov and search for "1031 exchanges" to find publications, forms, and explanations of the rules for like-kind exchanges of real estate.

adjusted purchase price of $105,000 and sell it at an adjusted sales price of $135,000, you have a taxable profit of $30,000. If you complete a like-kind exchange and meet all of the requirements, however, you can defer this tax. You may buy a replacement property for $142,000. In this case, the basis of the new property would be $112,000 or $30,000 less than the adjusted basis without the tax deferral:

Adjusted purchase price, replacement property	$142,000
Adjusted sales price, original property	$135,000
Less: Adjusted purchase price	−105,000
Deferred gain	−30,000
Net basis, replacement property	$112,000

Another way that you can save on taxes is by selling your primary residence. Under the rules, you can sell your home and the profits are tax free up to $500,000 (for a married couple filing jointly) or $250,000 (for single people). This has ramifications for real estate investors.

You can flip properties by buying one and selling another. This replacement approach assumes that property values are rising, that you are willing to move, and that the savings in taxes are high enough to justify the strategy. You can sell a primary residence as often as every 24 months, without limit. The only requirement is that the property you sell was your primary residence for at least 24 months during the past five years.

Say you bought your current home four years ago and have lived in it continuously. The price was $99,500 and you can sell today for $145,000. At the same time, you find a property you would like to buy

---

Key Point

The provision allowing you to sell your primary residence tax free opens up many possibilities for property flipping. If you are willing to move every two years, you can flip properties and never pay taxes on your profits.

Valuable Resource
Federal rules allow you to avoid taxes on primary residences you've lived in at least 24 months. However, state tax rules vary. To find out about real estate tax rules in any state, check the website www.state taxcentral.com.

for $126,000—and you believe it is a great value. In fact, you would buy and flip that property. At the same time you see an opportunity to perform a longer-term flip involving both properties—and all tax free. If you sell your current residence, your $45,500 profit is completely tax free. If you believe you could make the same profit by flipping the second property, you need to also realize that it would be taxable as an investment.

An alternative is to sell your current residence and take the tax-free profits, and move to the new property. As long as you remain there at least two years, you can repeat the process, selling the property tax free and finding a new, undervalued property to move to. This can be continued indefinitely, with none of your profits taxed along the way.

Conclusion

The tax rules for property flipping and investing are complicated. With the help of a qualified tax specialist, they are manageable. When you take into account the tax benefits derived from investing in real estate, you realize that few other investments can match them. These benefits include:

1. Deductibility of depreciation.
2. Deductibility of other expenses such as insurance, interest, and utilities.
3. Up to $25,000 annual loss deductions for passive activity (not allowed for any other kinds of passive activity).
4. Unlimited loss deductions for real estate professionals who meet all qualifications.
5. The ability to defer gains on all real estate profits by using like-kind exchange rules.

6. Tax-free sale of a primary residence as long as it was occupied at least 24 out of the last 60 months.

Real estate is an exceptionally good investment for anyone needing tax deductions. At the same time, real estate has historically outperformed inflation and beaten the stock market in terms of annual returns. While many worry about real estate bubbles after years of rapid market value increases in some areas, that problem is regional in nature. It is unlikely that a bubble will burst everywhere at once. All real estate markets are local in nature, so prices in your town will not slow down or drop just because the bubble bursts in Florida, New York, or California. Such events might affect the rate of change in market values elsewhere, but bubbles are not universal.

As long as you apply sensible standards for evaluating real estate and as long as you can find property flipping bargains, real estate remains one of the greatest potential markets for building wealth, offering low risk and consistent returns over many years.

Glossary

accelerated depreciation a calculation allowed for some assets in which more depreciation is claimed in earlier years and less in later years.

active participation status of a real estate investor. If the individual makes management decisions concerning properties, he or she is allowed to deduct up to $25,000 in annual losses from real estate investing.

activity under the federal tax rules, the nature of investment that determines how much you may deduct in losses. This determination is based on time you spend on investments and the degree of control you have over decisions.

adjusted gross income (AGI) for federal tax purposes, total taxable income reduced by specific adjustments but before calculating exemptions, itemized or standard deductions.

adjusted purchase price the stated and agreed-upon price paid for property, plus expenses related to the closing process, financing, and proration of expenses.

adjusted sales price the negotiated sales price, minus the seller's closing costs including commissions, taxes, recording fees, and inspection fees.

allocation an expanded version of diversification in which capital is invested in different markets, such as stocks, bonds, and real estate. The purpose in allocation is to avoid a negative impact on the entire portfolio if and when a particular market suffers a downturn.

annual percentage rate (APR) the actual interest a borrower is obligated to repay annually on a mortgage loan.

annualized return the comparative profit from an investment expressed as if the holding period were exactly one year.

anticipation the tendency of markets to demonstrate price trends due to the expectation of future events or changes.

appraisal a process of evaluation of a property for the purpose of estimating current market value. This is based on a study of replacement cost as well as market value of comparable properties in the same area or in similar areas.

assessor a city or county employee responsible for setting property values for the purpose of setting property tax liabilities.

balloon mortgage a mortgage in which interest-only payments are made for a term of months or years, and the entire principal balance is due in full at the end of the term.

bankable reference to a property's qualification for financing based on a lender's requirements, usually due to structural minimum rules.

basis   the adjusted purchase price of property or the value used to calculate net gain upon sale. The basis is subtracted from the adjusted sales price to arrive at the true cash-based profit on the sale.

bilateral contract   a type of contract in which both sides are required to perform; for example, a buyer agrees to pay for property, and a seller agrees to relinquish title.

book value   the net value of an asset, representing its purchase value minus depreciation.

breakeven cash flow   a condition in which rental income from property matches the sum of all cash outlays, including mortgage interest and principal, insurance, taxes, utilities, maintenance, and other expenses.

breakeven term   the number of months required in a replacement mortgage to offset the closing costs incurred.

bridge loan   a type of loan intended to serve as a short-term replacement for longer-term and more permanent financing, or to carry the mortgage debt for a short period of ownership in property.

built-up equity   the equity in real estate accumulated through growth in market value and, as a secondary source, in payments against outstanding mortgage loan balances.

bundled lots   several properties acquired at discount and offered for sale in a single transaction.

buy-and-hold strategy   a strategy for acquiring real estate in which property is acquired and rented out, to be sold when prices are higher. In the ideal buy-and-hold situation, rent is adequate to make mortgage payments and to pay for property taxes, insurance, utilities, and maintenance costs.

buyer's agent   a real estate agent who works for the buyer rather than for the seller, and who is compensated by a fee rather than through commissions.

capital expenditure   amounts spent to improve or maintain property, which have value beyond the current year. These expenditures are treated as long-term assets and have to be depreciated over many years.

cash flow   the movement of money in and out of an investment. In real estate, cash flow is of greater concern than ultimate profits. For example, speculators seek extremely short-term investments so that cash flow concerns are limited; therefore, they desire to sell properties as soon as possible after acquiring them.

cash flow risk   a form of risk involving the use of leverage. The greater the leverage used in investments, the greater the cash flow risk.

cash-based profit   a calculation of profit from property flipping based solely on a comparison between cash invested upon purchase and cash received upon sale.

change   a factor affecting valuation, based on the inevitable movement of trends of many types within the economic cycle.

comparable properties   in appraisal, properties that are found in the same neighborhood or in similar neighborhoods and sharing the same features as a property being appraised.

comparative analysis a technique in which two or more investments are compared using the same basic assumptions such as annualized yield. This is used in comparing final outcomes and for judging investment potential in advance.

competition the economic driving force creating growth or decline in market value of property. Greater competition for scarcer land drives prices up, and a lack of interest (low competition) in a type of property brings prices down.

conformity a principle of valuation; properties similar in size, age, condition, numbers of rooms, and amount of land tend to change in price in a uniform manner. Properties that do not conform to typical properties in the same area will not grow at the same rate as conforming properties.

contingent equity interest the interest a tenant has in a property when part of a lease option, which is strengthened as property values rise; or the interest that any owner of an option has in property based on growing market value and potential exercise.

contribution the principle stating that improvements add value as a factor of supply and demand, and not based on actual cost of those improvements.

cost method an appraisal method used to estimate what it would cost to duplicate a house as it stands today.

dealer an individual who buys real estate at a discount, marks it up, and sells at retail, profiting from the difference; or who act as go-between in the capacity of a licensed real estate agent or broker, compensated by commissions.

depreciation a reduction in the current cost or replacement value of property to reflect true value based on condition.

discount point a loan discount; a point charged in exchange for a reduced rate on a mortgage loan.

distressed properties any properties needing repairs, often of a serious nature; or those properties whose owners are experiencing financial problems or urgency to sell.

diversification a strategy for spreading risk, in which investment capital is placed in dissimilar products. The purpose of diversification is to ensure that bad news will not affect the entire portfolio in the same way.

earnest money a deposit made by a purchaser as part of a real estate contract to establish his or her seriousness about the deal. If the buyer backs out of the contract, the earnest money deposit is forfeited.

economic life an estimate of a property's potential life based on quality of construction, depreciation, and any upgraded or renovated areas.

effective age the age of a property based not on actual years since it was built, but on current condition; used to calculate annual depreciation from cost or replacement value.

elections decisions allowed under the rules to claim depreciation at a slower rate than provided under the rules, or to pick different depreciation methods. Most elections are irrevocable once made.

entry strategy   the identification of type, price, location, and holding period that will be employed in property flipping or in any type of investment.

exchange-traded funds (ETFs)   mutual funds with preidentified portfolios specializing in an industry or investing in stocks of a particular region or country. An ETF specializing in real estate companies offers one way of diversified equity investing without the use of leverage. ETF shares are traded over public exchanges, rather than bought or sold through the mutual fund itself.

fixed-rate mortgages   financing for real estate based on an interest rate that does not change over the entire term. For example, a 30-year, fixed-rate mortgage will maintain the same interest rate throughout the term.

fixer-upper   a property purchased primarily to upgrade through repairs, with the idea of spending minimum cash on cosmetic changes and then selling for a profit.

floor rate   the minimum interest rate that is charged on a variable-rate loan, even if the underlying index would take the rate below the floor level.

FSBO   Acronym meaning "for sale by owner," status of properties placed on the market directly by their owners and excluding real estate agents.

good-faith estimate   an estimate of a buyer's financing-related closing costs, required by the Real Estate Procedures Closing Act (RESPA).

gross rent multiplier (GRM)   a calculation used by appraisers as part of the income approach. The sales prices of other income properties are divided by income to arrive at GRM; then the average GRM factor is multiplied by rents in the subject property to arrive at value.

highest and best use   a principle of valuation, stating that real estate values are at a maximum when land is used in the most effective manner possible, given its features.

home equity line of credit (HELOC)   a secured line of credit based on your home equity; the borrower pays interest only when funds are drawn, and is allowed to repay borrowed amounts as quickly as possible without penalty.

impact fee   a fee charged to buyers when the property is part of a condo or co-op development; also called a *transfer fee*.

income approach   an appraisal method used for valuation of investment properties and based on income potential of comparable properties in the same area. The income approach is based on development of a gross rent multiplier (GRM), which is then applied against the subject property to estimate market value.

interest risk   the risk that interest rates will rise, which has an immediate effect on real estate values. Higher interest rates also affect property flipping because higher rates slow down the market.

interest-only loan   a mortgage loan requiring interest payments only and no reduction in principal. An interest-only loan usually also requires payment at a specified due date in the future.

inventory of properties   the number of properties currently listed and for sale divided by the average number of sales per month in a specific region or city; the lower the inventory, the stronger the market.

lease option a contract between a property owner and a tenant (or prospective buyer). The lease is a rental contract and the option grants the right to the leaseholder to purchase property at a fixed price before the expiration date.

leverage an investment strategy in which a portion of equity is augmented through borrowings to purchase more expensive items than the investor could afford in cash. In real estate, mortgage loans are the best-known form of leverage.

lifetime cap a clause in a variable-rate loan defining the maximum interest rate increase a lender can add to the beginning balance over the entire period of the loan.

like-kind exchange a trade of one investment property for another, allowing investors to pay taxes on profits in the future rather than in the year of sale.

liquidity risk a form of risk involving cash flow and the availability of money. The risk is based on the need for regular income from investment real estate to make mortgage payments, ongoing expenses, and unexpected repairs. The greater the leverage employed in a real estate portfolio, the higher the liquidity risk.

loan discount a charge lenders assess to borrowers in exchange for a reduced interest rate on a mortgage loan; also called a *discount point*.

loan origination fee a charge by lenders, also called *points*, to cover the cost of processing the loan. Each point is usually equal to 1 percent of the amount being borrowed.

long-term capital gains any gains from investments that were held for 12 months or longer, which are taxed at lower rates than ordinary income or short-term capital gains (gains on investments owned for less than 12 months).

magic thinking a form of "casual reasoning" in which beliefs, unsupportable by science, replace reasoning. For example, people carry good luck tokens or wear "lucky" clothing. Applied to the mentally ill, magic thinking involves a belief in special power, such as the ability to wish someone dead. Applied to investors, magic thinking includes a belief that thinking the right thoughts may make an investment increase in value.

MAI the designation of a commercial real estate appraiser awarded to qualified members by the Appraisal Institute.

market or sales comparison approach an appraisal method used for residential properties involving a study between the subject property and other properties that sold recently in the same or similar neighborhoods and sharing the same or similar characteristics.

market risk the best-known type of investment risk—that prices will fall after money has been invested. Market (or price) risk applies in all markets. In real estate, the combination of market risk with timing often defines whether investments succeed or fail.

market value the current value of property; the price at which a buyer agrees to buy and a seller agrees to sell.

material participation the status of a full-time real estate professional who, if qualified, is allowed to deduct all real estate losses without limitation.

meeting of the minds the agreement between two sides in a contract, which can include the price, deadlines, and other terms needed to create a valid and binding contract.

midmonth convention a depreciation rule determining first-year depreciation for real estate. It is based on dividing the year into 24 half-months and calculating depreciation on the assumption that the purchase occurred halfway through the month of actual purchase.

Modified Accelerated Cost Recovery System (MACRS) the most commonly used system for calculating depreciation on investment and business assets, which includes defined periods over which depreciation applies and the depreciation methods to be used for each type of asset.

modified adjusted gross income reported adjusted gross income without certain deductions, such as IRA contributions, student loan interest, Social Security benefits, self-employment tax, and tuition. Adding these items back to AGI increases the modified AGI and may reduce allowable real estate loss deductions.

mortgage insurance a type of insurance charged by lenders to borrowers when down payment level is less than 20 percent of the purchase price. This policy protects the lender in case of default on the loan.

mortgage pool an investment program structured like a mutual fund but consisting of secured home mortgages rather than stocks or bonds.

negative amortization condition in a loan when monthly payments are lower than the monthly interest owed. As a consequence, the loan balance rises each month.

negative transition a change in neighborhoods in which properties are empty or abandoned, crime is rising, and property values are falling due to lack of care, high rates of absentee ownership, or other negative trends.

net profit the calculated profit based on a comparison between adjusted sales price and adjusted purchase price. The difference between the two is divided by the adjusted purchase price and expressed as a percentage.

nonconforming property any property whose features are dissimilar to other properties in the same area, including lot size, condition, number of rooms, overall square feet, or design. Market appreciation of nonconforming properties is inhibited by their dissimilar features or attributes.

option premium the amount paid by the person acquiring an option to the property owner. The premium is paid in exchange for fixing the price of property in the event the option is exercised.

ordinary income an individual's taxable income, subject to published rates and not qualified for lower rates applicable to long-term capital gains, or excluded from tax due to investment rules.

participation rules the activity investors exhibit in buying, holding, and selling real estate and in the amount of time spent, degree of control, and decision-making power.

passive loss the loss from investments in which the investor is not actively involved such as limited partnerships or real estate. Losses generally cannot be deducted but have to be carried forward and applied against future passive gains. One exception involves directly owned real estate; investors may deduct up to $25,000 per year in losses.

payment cap   a provision in a variable rate mortgage limiting the maximum payment a borrower is required to make.

plottage   the principle of valuation stating that uniformity in land zoning and use tends to hold and increase value, and inconsistent zoning and planning tends to adversely impact values.

points   charges by lenders for processing a mortgage loan. A point is equal to 1 percent of the amount being borrowed and is charged to the buyer.

pooled investment   an investment with the funds of many individuals combined to make purchases collectively, much like a mutual fund. Mortgage pools invest in bundles of secured real estate mortgages, and are offered to the public by quasi-governmental agencies such as GNMA and FNMA.

portfolio loan   a loan carried by a lender on its own books and with its own money loaned out, and not assigned to another lender or to a mortgage pool.

positive transition   a change in a neighborhood in which values are increasing due to renovation of existing homes, replacement of outdated properties, and other favorable change.

prepaid expenses   certain expenses required to be paid in advance by buyers, charged in escrow. For example, any insurance premiums will be charged in advance.

price trend   the historical prices of properties in a particular area, involving a period of 12 months or more. The trend is useful in judging how real estate prices are moving currently, and to anticipate future price ranges.

primary residence   for tax purposes, a person's residence for calculation of tax-free sales. A primary residence must be occupied for at least 24 months out of the past 60 months.

progression   the observation that a property's market value is likely to increase when it is located near similar properties of higher quality and whose market value is increasing.

property flipping   a form of speculation in real estate that involves a very short period of ownership. The flipper finds undervalued properties, improves value through cosmetic improvements in many instances, and then sells the property at a profit.

prorated expenses   any expenses shared between seller and buyer, with the total divided based on the number of days in the liability period.

proration   a process of splitting expenses such as taxes, insurance, and utilities between buyer and seller. These expenses are split based on the number of days.

purchase option   an option granting the option owner the right, but not the obligation, to purchase property at a specified price and by a specified time. If the option is not exercised by the date indicated, it expires and becomes worthless.

rate cap   a clause in a variable-rate loan defining the maximum interest rate increase a lender can place on a loan, including the frequency that changes can occur.

recovery period   one of several asset classifications used for calculating depreciation. For non–real estate depreciated over either five or seven years, accelerated depreciation is allowed. For real estate, only straight-line depreciation is permitted.

refinancing   the replacement of a current mortgage with another, for the purpose of getting a lower rate, reducing payments through an extended term, or accessing equity for other purposes.

regression   a valuation principle stating that a property's value may decline if and when other, similar properties in the same area are falling in value.

rental demand   the specific demand market for rentals, affected by the supply of rental houses and apartments. This market coexists with the larger housing market with its pricing trends; but renters react to different factors than homeowners, so the two markets may not necessarily move in the same direction.

replacement cost   an appraisal estimate of the cost to replace a home as it exists today, given the possibility of exceptional architecture or handcrafting.

RESPA   acronym for the Real Estate Procedures Closing Act, a federal law that requires lenders to provide borrowers with a good-faith estimate of loan costs.

retailer   an investor who purchases property on the open market, privately, or through a dealer, with the idea of flipping at a profit.

risk tolerance   the level of risk you are able to accept in a particular product or market, determined by personal income and net worth; experience; and investing goals, attitudes, and preferences.

scout   an individual who researches the market to locate property flipping opportunities, and then reports those opportunities to other investors.

secondary market   market consisting of quasi-governmental agencies that collect home mortgages; bundle them with other, similar mortgages; and sell shares to investors.

secured debts   all debts involving a form of collateral, such as mortgage loans, which are secured by the value of property. In comparison, risks are much higher for unsecured debts such as promissory notes or corporate debentures; in the event of default, unsecured debts are more difficult to collect.

service   in lending institutions, the collection, processing, and recordkeeping of mortgage loans, even after the loan has been assigned or sold to another lender or to a mortgage pool.

settlement statement   a document summarizing the entire real estate transaction and showing all exchanges of funds and payments between buyer and seller.

speculation   an investment strategy employed by short-term investors. These investors seek rapid turnover of investment funds as opposed to long-term investors, whose objectives are to buy and hold for many years.

spread   the percentage of difference between asked and sold price of real estate. To compute, divide the difference in the two values by the asked price and express the result as a percentage.

SRA   the designation of a residential real estate appraiser awarded to qualified members by the Appraisal Institute.

straight-line depreciation   a method of calculating depreciation in which the same amount is claimed each year until the asset has been fully depreciated.

subject property   the property being appraised.

substitution   the principle stating that a property's value and potential growth will be limited to the same factors in other, similar properties in the same or similar neighborhoods.

suitability   the appropriate matching of a particular investment strategy to an individual, based on experience, knowledge, income, assets, investment goals, age, and family status.

supply and demand   the market forces at work that control and create cyclical price changes and, to a degree, value of property. Growing supply causes prices to fall and growing demand causes prices to rise.

sweat equity   a property's equity that grows as the result of an owner's work to improve property value, as opposed to increases based on growing demand.

tax avoidance   the preplanning and timing of transactions to reduce tax liabilities or to maximize current-year loss deductions by matching them against gains.

tax deferral   a procedure allowing the delay of payment of tax this year, by carrying profits forward and applying them against replacement investment properties.

tax planning   the forward-looking estimate of tax liabilities and, for real estate investors, tax benefits arising from real estate activities, coordinating real estate timing and decision making with the rest of a person's portfolio and as part of overall income and tax status.

teaser rate   an exceptionally low initial interest rate offered with a variable rate mortgage, which is replaced in 6 to 12 months by a higher market rate.

ten valuation principles   the rules governing the ways that value of real estate evolves: anticipation, change, competition, conformity, contribution, highest and best use, plottage, progression, regression, and substitution.

time on the market   the number of months (or weeks) that properties remain for sale on average. This indicates the relative strength or weakness—and the recent changes in time on the market indicate a trend in supply and demand.

time risk   the risk in real estate that profits will not materialize in the desired time frame. In that case, investors either accept losses or convert properties to longer-term rentals.

title search   a closing cost charged to the buyer involving checking the county records for any undisclosed liens, mortgages, or judgments against the property.

transfer fee   another term for the impact fee charged to buyers in condo or co-op developments.

unilateral contract   a type of contract binding one side to perform but not the other. For example, if a seller is required to sell under the terms of a contract but the buyer is not required to buy, the agreement is unilateral.

useful life   an estimate of an asset's reasonable utility and the basis for calculating depreciation.

variable-rate mortgages   also called adjustable-rate mortgages (ARMs), these loans contain provisions for periodic changes in the interest rate based on one of several loan rate indexes.

Index